CONTENTS

MEAT PIES, QUICHES, & PIZZAS

BREADS, SCONES, & TEA BREADS

BAKED PUDDINGS & SWEET TARTS

EVERYDAY CAKES

COOKIES, BAR COOKIES, & BROWNIES

CELEBRATION & CREAM CAKES

Cleanliness in the Kitchen

It is well worth remembering that many foods can carry some form of bacteria. In most cases, the worst it will lead to is a bout of food poisoning or gastroenteritis, although for certain groups this can be more serious—the risk can be reduced or eliminated by good food hygiene and proper cooking.

Do not buy food that is past its sell-by date, and do not consume food that is past its use-by date. When buying food, use your eyes and nose. If the food looks tired, limp, or discolored, or it has a rank, acrid, or simply bad smell, do not buy or eat it under any circumstances.

Be sure to take special care when preparing raw meat and fish. A separate chopping board should be used for each; wash the knife, board, and your hands thoroughly before handling or preparing any other food.

Regularly clean, defrost and clear out the refrigerator or freezer—it is worth checking the packaging to see exactly how long each product is safe to freeze. Avoid handling food if suffering from an upset stomach, since bacteria can be passed through food preparation.

Dishtowels must be washed and changed regularly. Ideally, use paper towels, which can be thrown out after use. Dishtowels should be left to soak in bleach, then washed in hot water in a washing machine.

Keep the hands, cooking utensils, and food preparation surfaces clean, and do not allow pets to climb on to any work surfaces.

BUYING

Avoid bulk buying where possible, especially fresh produce such as meat, poultry, fish, fruit, and vegetables. Fresh foods lose their nutritional value rapidly, so buying a little at a time minimizes loss of nutrients. It also eliminates a packed refrigerator, which reduces the effectiveness of the refrigeration process.

When buying prepackaged goods such as cans or cartons of cream and yogurts, check that the packaging is intact and not damaged or pierced. Cans should not be dented, pierced, or rusty. Check the sell-by dates even for cans and packs of dry ingredients such as flour and rice. Store fresh foods in the refrigerator as soon as possible—not in the car or office.

When buying frozen foods, ensure that they are not heavily iced on the outside and the contents feel completely frozen. Make sure that the frozen foods have been stored in the cabinet at the correct storage level and the temperature is below 0° F. Pack in cool bags to transport home, and place in the freezer as soon as possible after purchase.

PREPARATION

Make sure that all work surfaces and utensils are clean and dry. Hygiene should be given priority at all times. Separate chopping boards should be used for raw and cooked meats, fish, and vegetables. Currently, a variety of good-quality plastic boards come in various designs and colors. This makes differentiating easier, and the plastic has the added hygienic advantage of being washable at high temperatures in the dishwasher. If using the board for fish, first wash in cold water, then in hot to prevent odor. Also, remember that knives and utensils should always be thoroughly cleaned after use.

When cooking, be particularly careful to keep cooked and raw food separate to avoid any contamination. It is worth washing all fruits and vegetables regardless of whether they are going to be eaten raw or lightly cooked. This rule should apply even to prewashed herbs and salads.

Do not reheat food more than once.

If using a microwave, always check that the food is piping hot all the way through. The food should reach 160° F, and needs to be cooked at that temperature for at least three minutes to ensure that all bacteria are killed.)

All poultry must be thoroughly thawed before using. Remove the food to be thawed from the freezer and place in a shallow dish to contain the juices. Leave the food in the refrigerator until it is completely thawed. A 3 lb. whole chicken will take about 26–30 hours to thaw. To speed up the process, immerse the chicken in cold water. However, make sure that the water is changed regularly. When the joints can move freely and no ice crystals remain in the cavity, the bird is completely thawed.

Once thawed, remove the wrapper and pat the chicken dry. Place the chicken in a shallow dish, cover lightly, and store as close to the base of the refrigerator as possible. The chicken should be cooked as soon as possible.

Some foods can be cooked from frozen, including many prepacked foods such as soups, sauces, casseroles, and breads. Where applicable, follow the manufacturers' directions.

Vegetables and fruits can also be cooked from frozen, but meats and fish should be thawed first. The only time food can be refrozen is when the food has been thoroughly thawed, then cooked. Once the food has cooled, then it can be frozen again. On such occasions the food can only be stored for one month.

All poultry and game (except for duck) must be cooked thoroughly. When cooked, the juices will run clear on the thickest part of the bird—the best area to try is usually the thigh. Other meats, like ground meat and pork, should be cooked all the way through. Fish should turn opaque, be firm in texture, and break easily into large flakes.

When cooking leftovers, make sure they are reheated until piping hot and that any sauce or soup reaches boiling point first.

STORING, REFRERATING, AND FREEZING

Meat, poultry, fish, seafood, and dairy products should all be refrigerated. The temperature of the refrigerator should be between 34–41° F while the freezer temperature should not rise above 0° F..

To ensure the optimum refrigerator and freezer temperature, avoid leaving the door open for a long time. Try not to overstock the refrigerator, since this reduces the airflow inside and reduces the effectiveness of cooling the food within.

When refrigerating cooked food, allow it to cool down quickly and completely before refrigerating. Hot food will raise the temperature of the refrigerator and possibly affect or spoil other food stored inside.

Food within the refrigerator and freezer should always be covered. Raw and cooked food should be stored in separate parts of the refrigerator. Cooked food should be kept on the top shelves of the refrigerator, while raw meat, poultry, and fish should be placed on bottom shelves to avoid drips and cross-contamination. It is recommended that eggs should be refrigerated in order to maintain their freshness and shelf life.

Take care that frozen foods are not stored in the freezer for too long. Blanched vegetables can be stored for one month; beef, lamb, poultry, and pork for six months; and unblanched vegetables and fruits in syrup for a year. Oily fish and sausages should be stored for three months. Dairy products can last four to six months, while cakes and pastries should be kept in the freezer for three to six months.

HIGH-RISK FOODS

Certain foods may carry risks to people who are considered vulnerable, such as the elderly, the ill, pregnant women, babies, young infants, and those with a compromised immune system.

It is advisable to avoid those foods listed below which belong to a higher-risk category.

There is a slight chance that some eggs carry the bacteria salmonella. To eliminate this risk, cook the eggs until both the yolk and the white are firm. Pay particular attention to dishes and products incorporating lightly cooked or raw eggs, which should be eliminated from the diet.

Sauces including Hollandaise, mayonnaise, mousses, soufflés, and meringues all use raw or lightly cooked eggs, as do custard-based dishes, ice creams, and sorbets. These are all considered high-risk foods to the vulnerable groups mentioned above.

Certain meats and poultry also carry the potential risk of salmonella and should be cooked thoroughly until the juices run clear and there is no pinkness left. Unpasteurized products such as milk, cheese (especially soft cheese), pâté, meat (both raw and cooked) all have the potential risk of listeria, and should be avoided.

When buying seafood, buy from a reputable source which has a high turnover, to ensure freshness. Fish should have bright, clear eyes, shiny skin, and bright pink or red gills. The fish should feel stiff to the touch, with a slight smell of sea air and iodine. The flesh of fish steaks and fillets should be translucent with no signs of discoloration. Mollusks such as scallops, clams, and mussels are sold fresh, and are still alive. Avoid any that are open or do not close when tapped lightly. In the same way, univalves should withdraw back into their shells when lightly prodded. When choosing cephalopods such as squid and octopus, they should have a firm flesh and pleasant sea smell.

As with all fish, whether it is shellfish or seafish, care is required when freezing. It is imperative to check whether the fish has been frozen before. If it has been frozen, then it should not be frozen again under any circumstances.

Essential Ingredients

The quantities may differ, but basic baking ingredients do not vary greatly. Let us take a closer look at the baking ingredients which are essential.

FAT

Butter and stick margarine are the fats most commonly used in baking. Others can also be used, such as shortening, lard, and oil. Low-fat spreads are not suitable for baking, as they break down when cooked at a high temperature. Often, it is a matter of personal preference which fat you choose when baking, but there are a few guidelines that are important to remember.

Sweet butter is the fat most commonly used in cake-making, especially in rich fruit cakes and the heavier sponge cakes, such as Madeiras or chocolate tortes. Sweet butter gives a distinctive flavor to the cake. Some people favor margarine, which imparts little or no flavor to the cake. As a rule, firm margarine and butter should not be used straight from the refrigerator, but allowed to come to room temperature before using. Also, fats should first be beaten alone before creaming or mixing. Soft margarine is best suited to one-stage recipes. If oil is used, care should be taken—it is a good idea to follow a specific recipe, as the proportions of oil to flour and eggs are different.

Fat is an integral ingredient when making pastry; again, there are a few specific guidelines to bear in mind.

For short pastry, the best results are achieved by using equal amounts of lard or shortening with butter or stick margarine. The amount of fat used is always half the amount of flour. Other pastries use differing amounts of ingredients. Pâté sucrée (a sweet flan pastry) uses all butter with eggs and a little sugar, while flaky or puff pastry uses a larger proportion of fat to flour and relies on the folding and rolling during mixing to ensure that the pastry rises and flakes well. When using a recipe, refer to the instructions to obtain the best results.

FLOUR

We can buy a wide range of flours, all designed for specific jobs. Bread flour, which is rich in gluten whether it is white or brown (this includes granary and stone-ground), is best kept for bread and Yorkshire pudding. It is also recommended for steamed suet puddings, as well as puff pastry. Type 00 flour is designed for pasta-making, and there is no substitute for this flour. Ordinary or all-purpose flour is best for cakes, cookies, and sauces, which absorb the fat easily and give a soft, light texture. This flour comes in plain white or self-rising, as well as whole-wheat. Self-rising flour, which has the leavening agent already incorporated, is best kept for sponge cakes, where it is important that an even rising is achieved. All-purpose flour can be used for all types of baking and sauces. If using all-purpose flour for cookies or cakes and puddings, unless otherwise stated in the

recipe, use 1 teaspoon of baking powder to 2 cups of flour. With sponge cakes and light fruit cakes, it is best to use self-rising flour, as the leavening agent has already been added to the flour. This way, there is no danger of using too much flour, which can result in a sunken cake with a sour taste. There are other rising agents that are also used. Some cakes use baking soda with or without cream of tartar, blended with warm or sour milk. Beaten eggs also act as a rising agent, since the air trapped in the egg ensures that the mixture rises. Generally no other leavening agent is required.

Also, it is possible to buy flours that contain no gluten. For example, buckwheat, soy, and chickpea flours.

EGGS

When a recipe states 1 egg, it is generally accepted that this refers to a large egg (24 oz. per dozen.) Eggs come in a variety of sizes, however, and sometimes when baking, a recipe will state the egg size that should be used. The other eggs sizes available, based on their minimum weight per dozen, are: jumbo (30 oz.), extra large (27 oz.), medium (21 oz.), small (18 oz.), and peewee (15 oz.).

Most hens' eggs on the market have been graded according to quality and size under USDA standards. Eggs are graded AA, A, and B, and the classification is determined by interior and exterior quality.

Interior quality is judged by "candling," an electronic method where the eggs roll over high-intensity lights to allow their insides to be examined. Originally, the eggs where held up to a candle to be inspected, hence the name "candling." The quality of the interior of an egg is determined by the size of the air cell (the space at the large end of the egg between the white and shell), the density and quantity of the white, and whether the yolk is firm and free

the rolling pin, lift the remaining pastry, and cover the pie dish. Press together, then seal. Using a sharp knife, trim off any excess pastry from around the edges. Try to avoid brushing the edges of the pastry, especially puff pastry, since this prevents the pastry from rising evenly. Before placing in the oven, make a small hole in the center of the pie to allow the steam to escape.

The edges of the pie can be forked by pressing the back of a fork around the edge of the pie, or instead crimp by pinching the edge crust, holding the thumb and forefinger of your right hand against the edge while gently pushing with the forefinger of your left hand. Other ways of finishing the pie are knocking up (achieved by gently pressing your forefinger down on to the rim and, at the same time, tapping a knife horizontally along the edge, giving it a flaky appearance), or fluting the edges by pressing your thumb down on the edge of the pastry while gently drawing back an all-purpose knife about ½ inch and repeating around the rim. Experiment by putting leaves and berries made out of leftover pastry to finish off the pie, then brush the top of the pie with beaten egg.

LINING CAKE PANS

If a recipe states that the pan needs lining, do not be tempted to ignore this. Rich fruit cakes and other cakes that take a long time to cook benefit from the pan being lined so that the edges and base do not burn or dry out. Waxed or baking parchment is ideal for this. It is a good idea to have the paper at least double thickness, or preferably 3–4 thicknesses. Sponge cakes and other cakes that are cooked in 30 minutes or less are also better if the bases are lined, since it is far easier to remove them from the pan.

The best way to line a round or square pan is to lightly draw around the base and then cut just inside the markings, making it easy to sit in the pan. Next, lightly grease the paper so it easily peels away from the cake. If the sides of the pan also need to be lined, then cut a strip of paper long enough for the pan. This can be measured by wrapping a piece of string around the rim of the pan. Once again, lightly grease the paper, push against the pan, and grease once more, since this will hold the paper to the sides of the pan. Steamed puddings usually need only a disk of waxed paper at the bottom of the dish, as the sides come away easily.

HINTS FOR SUCCESSFUL BAKING

Make sure that the ingredients are accurately measured. A cake that has too much flour or insufficient egg will be dry and crumbly. Take care when measuring the leavening agent, if used, since too much will mean that the cake will rise too quickly and then sink. Insufficient rising agent means the cake will not rise in the first place.

Make sure that the oven is preheated to the correct temperature; it can take 10 minutes to reach 350° F. You may find that an oven thermometer is a good investment. Cakes are best if baked in the center of the preheated oven. Do not open the oven door at the beginning of baking, as a draft can make the cake sink. If using a convection oven, then refer to the manufacturers' instructions, as they normally cook 10-20° hotter than conventional ovens.

Check that the cake is thoroughly cooked by removing from the oven and inserting a clean skewer into the cake. Leave for about 30 seconds, then remove. If the skewer is completely clean, then the cake is done: if there is a little mixture left on the skewer, then return the cake to the oven for a few minutes.

Other problems that you may encounter while cake-making are insufficient creaming of the fat and sugar, or a curdled, creamed mixture (which will result in a densely textured and often fairly solid cake). Flour that has not been folded in carefully enough or has not been mixed with enough rising agent may also result in a fairly heavy consistency. It is very important to make sure that the correct size of pan is used, since you may end up either with a flat, hard cake or one that has spilled over the edge of the pan. Another tip to be aware of (especially when cooking with fruit) is that if the consistency is too soft, the cake will not be able to support the fruit.

Finally, when you take your cake out of the oven, unless the recipe states that it should be left in the pan until cold, leave for a few minutes, then loosen the edges and turn out onto a wire rack to cool. Cakes that are left in the pan for too long, unless otherwise stated, tend to sink or slightly overcook.

When storing, make sure the cake is completely cool before placing it into an airtight plastic container.

Culinary Terms Explained

BAIN MARIE A French term, meaning "water bath." Refers to a shallow pan, often a roasting pan, half-filled with water. Smaller dishes of food are then placed in it, allowing them to cook at lower temperatures without overheating. This method is often used to cook custards and other egg dishes, or to keep some dishes warm.

BAKING BLIND The method often used for cooking the pastry shell for flans and tarts before the filling is added. After lining the pan with the uncooked pastry, it is then covered with a sheet of waxed paper or baking parchment and weighed down with either ceramic baking beans or dried beans (or sometimes rice), and is baked in the oven as directed.

BAKING PARCHMENT
Used for wrapping food to be cooked (*en papillote*) and for lining cake pans to prevent the cake from sticking to the pan.

BAKING POWDER A leavening agent which works by producing carbon dioxide as a consequence of a reaction caused by the acid and alkali ingredients, which expand during the baking process and make the breads and cakes rise.

BAKING SODA When combined with liquid, baking soda acts as a raising agent.

BEATING The method by which air is introduced into a mixture using a fork, wooden spoon, whisk, or electric mixer. Beating is also used as a method to soften ingredients.

BINDING Adding liquid or egg to bring a dry mixture together. Normally, this entails using either a fork, spoon, or your fingertips.

BLENDER An electric machine with rotating blades used mainly with soft and wet ingredients to purée and liquidize, although it can also grind dry ingredients such as nuts and bread crumbs.

BLENDING Dry ingredients are mixed with liquid to form a smooth paste, used for thickening stews, casseroles, soups, and sauces.

BRIOCHE A traditional bread eaten in France for breakfast, usually served warm. Brioche has a rich, breadlike texture, contains yeast, and is baked in the shape of a small, round loaf. A delicious substitute for bread in bread and butter pudding.

CARAMEL Obtained by heating sugar at a very low heat until it turns liquid and deep brown in color. Caramel is used in dishes such as crème caramel, which is, in turn, baked in a bain marie.

CHOUX A type of pastry (rather like a glossy batter) that is piped into small balls on to a baking sheet and baked until light and airy. They can then be filled with cream or savory fillings.

COCOTTE Another name for a ramekin (a small, ovenproof, earthenware pot used for individual portions).

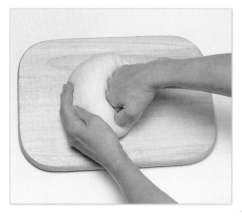

CORNSTARCH Used to thicken, and can also be used in meringue making to keep the meringue from becoming hard and brittle, and to enhance its texture.

CREAM OF TARTAR Another leavening agent often present in both self-rising flour and baking powder.

CREAMING The method by which fat and sugar are beaten together until lighter in color and fluffy. By creaming the fat in cake mixtures, air is incorporated into the fairly high fat content. It therefore lightens the texture of cakes and puddings.

CRIMPING The fluted effect used for the decoration on pies or tarts, created by pinching the edge crust while holding the thumb and forefinger of your right hand against the edge and gently pushing with the forefinger of your left hand.

CRUMB The term by which flour and fat are combined, typically for use in pastry, crumble, and cookies.

CURDLE When the milk separates from a sauce through acidity or excessive heat. This can also happen to creamed cake mixtures that have separated due to the eggs being too cold or added too quickly.

DARIOLE A small, narrow mold with sloping sides used for making Madeleines. They can also be used for individual puddings, and molded gelatin desserts.

DOUGH A dense mixture of flour, water, and, often, yeast. Also used to describe raw pastry, and cookie mixtures.

DREDGING The sprinkling of food with a coating (generally of flour or sugar). A board may be dredged with flour before the pastry is rolled out, and cakes and cookies can be dredged with sugar or confectioners' sugar after baking.

DROPPING CONSISTENCY The consistency to which a cake or pudding mixture reaches before being cooked. It tends to be fairly soft (but not runny), and should drop off a spoon in about five seconds when tapped lightly on the side of a bowl.

DUST To sprinkle lightly, often with flour, sugar, or confectioners' sugar.

EN CROÛTE Used to describe food that is covered with raw pastry and then baked.

EN PAPILLOTE A French term used to describe food that is baked, but is wrapped in waxed paper or baking parchment before cooking. This works well with fish, since the aroma from the different herbs or spices and the fish are contained during cooking and not released until the paper package is opened.

FAHRENHEIT (° F) A scale for measuring the temperature of the oven.

FERMENTING A term used during bread, beer, or wine making to note the chemical change brought about through the use of a fermenting agent, such as yeast.

FOLDING A method of combining creamed fat and sugar with flour in cake and pudding mixes, usually by carefully mixing with a large metal spoon, either by cutting and folding, or by doing a figure-eight in order to maintain a light texture.

GLACÉ A French term meaning "glossy" or "iced." Glacé icing is a quick icing often used to decorate cakes and biscuits. It is made using confectioners' sugar and warm water.

GRINDING Reducing hard ingredients, such as nuts to crumbs, normally by the use of a grinder or a mortar and pestle.

KNEAD The process of pummeling and working dough in order to strengthen the gluten in the flour and make the dough more elastic, thus allowing it to rise better. In pastry making, the dough is kneaded on a lightly floured surface to give a smooth and elastic pastry, making it easier to roll and ensuring an even texture after baking. In both cases, the outside of the dough is drawn into the center.

PASTEURIZING The term given when milk and eggs are heated to destroy bacteria.

PHYLLO A type of pastry that is wafer-thin. Three to four sheets are usually used at a time in baking.

PIPING The way in which cakes and desserts are decorated, or the method by which choux pastry is placed onto a cookie sheet. This is achieved by putting cream, frosting, or mixture in a nylon bag (with a nozzle attached) and then slowly forcing through the nozzle and piping it onto the cake or baking tray.

PROOFING The term used in bread making when the bread is allowed to rise a second time after it has been kneaded once and then shaped before it is baked.

PUFF PASTRY Probably the richest of pastries. When making from scratch, it requires the lightest of handling.

RAMEKIN An ovenproof, earthenware dish which provides an individual serving.

RICE PAPER Edible paper made from the pith of a Chinese tree; it can be used as a base on which to bake sticky cakes and cookies such as almond macaroons.

RUBBING IN The method of combining fat into flour for crumble toppings, short-crust pastry, biscuits, and cookies.

SCALLOPING The term given to a type of pie decoration achieved by horizontal cuts made in the pastry, which is then pulled back with the knife to produce a scalloped effect.

SIFTING The shaking of dry ingredients (primarily flour) through a metal or nylon sieve to remove impurities before using in baking. Quantities of flour may also be lightened by using a flour sifter.

UNLEAVENED Often refers to bread which does not use a leavening agent and is therefore flat, such as pita bread.

VOL-AU-VENT Meaning "to fly on the wind," this small and usually round or oval puff pastry case is first baked, and then filled with savory meat, seafood, or vegetable filling in a sauce.

WAXED PAPER Semitransparent paper with a thin coating of wax on each side. Because it is moisture-proof and nonstick, it is extremely useful when baking for lining cake pans. Traditionally, it was used to cover foods, but today most people tend to use plastic wrap or aluminum foil.

WHIPPING/WHISKING The term given to incorporating air rapidly into a mixture (either through using a manual whisk or an electric mixer).

ZEST Very thin, long pieces of the colored part of an orange, lemon, or lime peel, containing the fruit oil that is responsible for the citrus flavor. Normally, a zester is used to remove the zest without any of the bitter white pith. (Rind refers to the peel which has been grated on a grater into very small pieces.)

Finnan Haddie Tart

1 Preheat the oven to 375° F. Sift the flour and salt into a large bowl. Add the fats and mix lightly. Using the fingertips, rub into the flour until the mixture resembles bread crumbs.

2 Sprinkle 1 tablespoon of cold water into the mixture and, with a knife, start bringing the dough together. (It may be necessary to use the hands for the final stage.) If the dough does not form a ball instantly, add a little more water.

3 Put the pastry in a plastic bag and chill for at least 30 minutes.

4 On a lightly floured surface, roll out the pastry and use to line a 7-inch, lightly greased quiche or tart pan. Prick the base all over with a fork and bake blind in the preheated oven for 15 minutes.

5 Carefully remove the pastry from the oven, then brush with a little of the beaten egg.

6 Return to the oven for an additional 5 minutes, then place the fish in the pastry shell.

7 For the filling, beat together the eggs and cream. Add the mustard, black pepper, and cheese, and pour over the fish.

8 Sprinkle with the chives and bake for 35–40 minutes or until the filling is golden brown and set in the center. Serve hot or cold with the lemon and tomato wedges and salad leaves.

INGREDIENTS
Serves 6

FLAKY PASTRY:

1 cup all-purpose flour
pinch of salt
2 tbsp. lard or shortening, cut into small cubes
3 tbsp. butter or margarine, cut into small cubes

FOR THE FILLING:

½ lb. smoked haddock, skinned and cubed
2 large eggs, beaten
1 cup heavy cream
1 tsp. Dijon mustard
freshly ground black pepper
1 cup Swiss cheese, grated
1 tbsp. freshly cut chives

TO SERVE:

lemon wedges
tomato wedges
green salad

Food Fact

Named after the Scottish fishing village of Findon, Finnan Haddie is a lightly smoked haddock popular for breakfast in the U.K. Smoked salmon may be substituted.

Stilton, Tomato, & Zucchini Quiche

1 Preheat the oven to 375° F. On a lightly floured surface, roll out the pastry and use to line a 7-inch, lightly greased quiche or flan pan, trimming any excess pastry with a knife.

2 Prick the base all over with a fork and bake blind in the preheated oven for 15 minutes. Remove the pastry from the oven and brush with a little of the beaten egg. Return to the oven for an additional 5 minutes.

3 Heat the butter in a skillet and gently fry the onion and zucchini for about 4 minutes until soft and starting to brown. Transfer into the pastry shell.

4 Sprinkle the Stilton cheese over evenly, and top with the halved cherry tomatoes. Beat together the eggs and crème fraîche, and season to taste with salt and pepper.

5 Pour the filling into the pastry shell and bake in the oven for 35–40 minutes or until the filling is golden brown and set in the center. Serve the quiche hot or cold.

INGREDIENTS
Serves 4

1 quantity flaky pastry (see page 16)

2 tbsp. butter

1 onion, peeled and finely chopped

1 zucchini, trimmed and sliced

4 oz. Stilton cheese, crumbled (if not available, substitute Roquefort or another blue-veined cheese)

6 cherry tomatoes, halved

2 large eggs, beaten

1 scant cup crème fraîche (if not available, substitute sour cream)

salt and freshly ground black pepper

Food Fact

Stilton is a very traditional British cheese that often makes an appearance on the cheese board or served with a plowman's lunch in a pub. It gets much of its full, pungent flavor from its veins (created from the steel wires that are inserted into the cheese during the maturing process). It is worth looking for a piece of Stilton with a lot of veins that has been matured for a longer time.

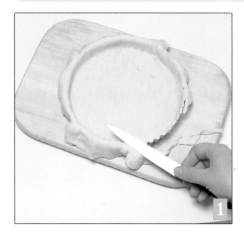

French Onion Tart

1 Preheat the oven to 400° F. Place the butter in the freezer for 30 minutes. Sift the flour and salt into a large bowl. Remove the butter from the freezer and grate, using the coarse side of a grater, dipping the butter in the flour every now and then to make it easier to grate.

2 Mix the butter into the flour using a knife, making sure that all of the butter is coated thoroughly with flour.

3 Add 2 tablespoons of cold water and continue to mix, bringing the mixture together. Use your hands to complete the mixing. Add a little more water if needed to leave a clean bowl. Place the pastry in a plastic bag and chill in the refrigerator for 30 minutes.

4 Heat the oil in a large skillet, then fry the onions for 10 minutes, stirring occasionally until softened.

5 Stir in the white wine vinegar and sugar. Increase the heat and stir frequently, for another 4–5 minutes until the onions turn a deep caramel color. Cook for another 5 minutes, then set aside to cool.

6 On a lightly floured surface, roll out the pastry to a 14-inch circle. Wrap over a rolling pin and move the circle onto a cookie sheet.

7 Sprinkle half the cheese over the pastry, leaving a 2-inch border around the edge, then spoon the caramelized onions over the cheese.

8 Fold the uncovered pastry edges over the edge of the filling to form a rim, and brush the rim with beaten egg or milk.

9 Season to taste with salt and pepper. Sprinkle over the remaining cheddar cheese and bake for 20–25 minutes. Transfer to a large plate and serve immediately.

INGREDIENTS
Serves 4

QUICK FLAKY PASTRY:
½ cup butter
1½ cups all-purpose flour
pinch of salt

FOR THE FILLING:
2 tbsp. olive oil
4 large onions, peeled and thinly sliced
3 tbsp. white wine vinegar
2 tbsp. dark brown sugar
a little beaten egg or milk
1½ cups cheddar cheese, grated
salt and freshly ground black pepper

Tasty Tip

For a milder, nutty taste, replace the cheddar cheese with Swiss cheese and grate a little nutmeg over the layer of cheese in step 7.

Beef & Red Wine Pie

1 Preheat the oven to 400° F. Toss the beef cubes in the seasoned flour.

2 Heat the oil in a large heavy-based skillet. Fry the beef in batches for about 5 minutes until golden brown.

3 Return all of the beef to the pan and add the onions, garlic, and thyme. Fry for about 10 minutes, stirring occasionally. If the beef begins to stick, add a little water.

4 Add the red wine and stock, and bring to a boil. Stir in the Worcestershire sauce, ketchup, and bay leaves.

5 Cover and simmer on a very low heat for about 1 hour or until the beef is tender.

6 Heat the butter and gently sauté the mushrooms until golden brown. Add to the stew. Simmer uncovered for an additional 15 minutes. Remove the bay leaves. Spoon the beef into a 1-quart pie dish and set aside.

7 Roll out the pastry on a lightly floured surface. Cut out the lid to ¼ inch wider than the dish. Brush the rim with the beaten egg and lay the pastry lid on top. Press to seal, then seal the edges with the back of a knife.

8 Cut a slit in the lid and brush with the beaten egg or milk to glaze. Bake in the preheated oven for 30 minutes or until golden. Garnish with the sprig of parsley and serve immediately.

INGREDIENTS
Serves 4

1 quantity quick flaky pastry (see page 20), chilled
1½ lbs. round steak, cubed
4 tbsp. seasoned all-purpose flour
2 tbsp. sunflower oil
2 onions, peeled and chopped
2 garlic cloves, peeled and crushed
1 tbsp. freshly chopped thyme
1¼ cups red wine
⅔ cup beef stock
1–2 tsp. Worcestershire sauce
2 tbsp. ketchup
2 bay leaves
1 tbsp. butter
button mushrooms
beaten egg or milk, to glaze
sprig of parsley, to garnish

Helpful Hint

Flaky or puff pastry could also be used to top the pie in this recipe. It is important, though, whichever pastry is used, to brush the top with beaten egg or milk before baking, as this will result in an appetizing golden crust.

Moroccan Lamb with Apricots

1 Preheat the oven to 375° F. Pound the ginger, garlic, cardamom, and cumin to a paste with a mortar and pestle. Heat 1 tablespoon of the oil in a large skillet, and fry the spice paste for 3 minutes. Remove and set aside.

2 Add the remaining oil and fry the lamb in batches for about 5 minutes until golden brown. Return all the lamb to the pan and add the onions and spice paste. Fry for 10 minutes, stirring occasionally.

3 Add the chopped tomatoes, cover, and simmer for 15 minutes. Add the apricots and chickpeas, and simmer for an additional 15 minutes.

4 Lightly grease a round 7-inch springform cake pan.

Lay one sheet of phyllo pastry in the base of the pan, allowing the excess to fall over the sides. Brush with melted butter, then layer five more sheets in the pan and brush each one with butter.

5 Spoon in the filling and level the surface. Layer half the remaining phyllo sheets on top, again brushing each with butter. Fold the overhanging pastry over the top of the filling. Brush the last sheet with butter, and place it on top of the pie so that the whole pie is completely covered. Brush with melted butter once more.

6 Bake in the preheated oven for 45 minutes, then set aside for 10 minutes. Remove the pie. Sprinkle with the nutmeg, garnish with dill sprigs, and serve.

INGREDIENTS
Serves 6

2-in. piece fresh ginger, peeled and grated
3 garlic cloves, peeled and crushed
1 tsp. ground cardamom
1 tsp. ground cumin
2 tbsp. olive oil
1 lb. leg of lamb, cubed
1 large red onion, peeled and chopped
1¼ cups canned, chopped tomatoes
¼ cup dried apricots
1¼ cups canned chickpeas, drained
7 large sheets phyllo pastry
4 tbsp. butter, melted
pinch of nutmeg
dill sprigs, to garnish

Food Fact

Phyllo pastry is sold rolled in wafer-thin sheets and is available from most supermarkets.

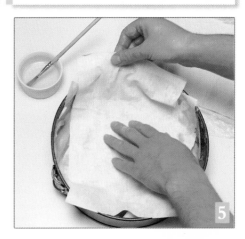

Bacon, Mushroom, & Cheese Puffs

1 Preheat the oven to 400° F. Heat the olive oil in a large skillet.

2 Add the mushrooms and bacon to the skillet, and fry for 6–8 minutes until golden in color. Stir in the chopped parsley, then season to taste with salt and pepper. Allow to cool.

3 Roll the sheet of pastry a little thinner on a lightly floured surface to a 12-inch square. Cut the pastry into 4 equal squares.

4 Stir the grated Swiss cheese into the mushroom mixture. Spoon a quarter of the mixture onto one half of each square.

5 Brush the edges of the square with a little of the beaten egg.

6 Fold over the pastry to form a triangular pocket. Seal the edges well and place on a lightly greased cookie sheet. Repeat until the squares are done.

7 Make shallow cuts in the top of the pastry with a knife.

8 Brush the pockets with the remaining beaten egg and cook in the preheated oven for 20 minutes or until puffy and golden brown.

9 Serve warm or cold, garnished with the arugula and served with tomatoes.

INGREDIENTS
Serves 4

1 tbsp. olive oil
field mushrooms, wiped and coarsely chopped
½ lb. bacon, coarsely chopped
2 tbsp. freshly chopped parsley
salt and freshly ground black pepper
¾ lb. ready-made puff pastry sheets, thawed if frozen
¼ cup Swiss cheese, grated
1 medium egg, beaten
arugula or watercress, to garnish
tomatoes, to serve

Tasty Tip

The Swiss cheese in this recipe can be replaced by any other cheese, but for best results, use a cheese such as cheddar, which, like Swiss cheese, melts easily! The bacon can also be replaced by slices of sweeter cured hams such as pancetta or prosciutto.

Fennel & Caramelized Shallot Tartlets

1 Preheat the oven to 400° F. Sift the flour into a bowl, then rub in the butter using your fingertips. Stir in the cheese, and add the egg yolk with about 2 tablespoons of cold water. Mix to a firm dough, then knead lightly. Wrap in plastic wrap and chill in the refrigerator for 30 minutes.

2 Roll out the pastry on a lightly floured surface and use to line 6 4-inch individual tartlet pans which are about ¾ inch deep.

3 Line the pastry crusts with waxed paper and fill with ceramic beans or rice. Bake blind in the preheated oven for about 10 minutes, then remove the paper and beans.

4 Heat the oil in a skillet, add the shallots and fennel, and fry gently for 5 minutes. Sprinkle with the sugar and cook for an additional 10 minutes, stirring occasionally until lightly caramelized. Set aside until cooled.

5 Beat together the egg and cream, and season to taste with salt and pepper. Divide the shallot mixture among the pastry crusts. Pour over the egg mixture and sprinkle with the cheese and cinnamon. Bake for 20 minutes until golden and set. Serve with the salad leaves.

INGREDIENTS
Serves 6

CHEESE PASTRY:
1½ cups all-purpose white flour
6 tbsp. salted butter
½ cup Swiss cheese, grated
1 small egg yolk

FOR THE FILLING:
2 tbsp. olive oil
½ lb. shallots, peeled and halved
1 fennel bulb, trimmed and sliced
1 tsp. brown sugar
1 medium egg
⅔ cup heavy cream
salt and freshly ground black pepper
¼ cup Swiss cheese, grated
½ tsp. ground cinnamon
mixed salad, to serve

Tasty Tip
Fennel has a very aromatic, almost aniseed flavor, which works particularly well with the sweet shallots and the cheese in this dish. A nice addition is to add a generous grating of nutmeg to the pie filling in step 5, since this complements the creamy cheese filling.

Fish Puff Tart

1 Preheat the oven to 425° F. On a lightly floured surface, roll out the pastry into an 8 x 10 inch rectangle.

2 Draw a 7 x 9 inch rectangle in the center of the pastry, to form a 1-inch border. (Be careful not to cut through the pastry.)

3 Lightly cut crisscross patterns in the border of the pastry with a knife.

4 Place the fish on a chopping board, and with a sharp knife, skin the cod and smoked haddock. Cut into thin slices.

5 Spread the pesto evenly over the bottom of the pastry shell with the back of a spoon.

6 Arrange the fish, tomatoes, and cheese in the pastry shell, and brush the pastry with the beaten egg.

7 Bake the tart in the preheated oven for 20–25 minutes until the pastry is well risen, puffed, and golden brown. Garnish with the chopped parsley and serve immediately.

INGREDIENTS
Serves 4

¾ lb. prepared puff pastry, thawed
  if frozen
5 oz. smoked haddock
5 oz. fresh cod
1 tbsp. pesto sauce
2 tomatoes, sliced
4 oz. goat cheese, sliced
1 medium egg, beaten
freshly chopped parsley, to garnish

Food Fact

The Scottish name for smoked haddock is *finnan haddie*, named after the Scottish fishing village of Findon, near Aberdeen. Smoked haddock has been a favorite breakfast dish in Findon and the rest of Scotland for many years. Although this type of fish was traditionally caught and smoked (sometimes over peat fires) in Scotland, today the fish is produced in New England and other Eastern coastal states of America.

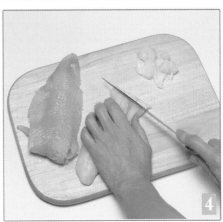

Spinach, Pine Nut, & Mascarpone Pizza

1 Preheat the oven to 400° F. Sift the flour and salt into a bowl, and stir in the yeast. Make a well in the center and gradually add the water and oil to form soft dough.

2 Knead the dough on a floured surface for about 5 minutes until smooth and elastic. Put in a lightly greased bowl and cover with plastic wrap. Leave to rise in a warm place for 1 hour.

3 Punch the pizza dough with your fist a few times, shape, and roll out thinly on a lightly floured board. Place on a lightly floured cookie sheet and lift the edge to make a little rim. Place another cookie sheet into the preheated oven to heat up.

4 Heat half the oil in a skillet, and gently fry the onion and garlic until soft and starting to change color.

5 Squeeze out any excess water from the spinach and chop finely. Add to the onion and garlic with the remaining olive oil. Season to taste with salt and pepper.

6 Spread the passata on the pizza dough and top with the spinach mixture. Mix the mascarpone with the pine nuts and dot over the pizza.

7 Slide the pizza onto the hot cookie sheet and bake for 15–20 minutes. Transfer to a large plate and serve immediately.

INGREDIENTS
Serves 2–4

BASIC PIZZA DOUGH:
2 cups bread flour
½ tsp. salt
¼ tsp. quick-acting dried yeast
⅔ cup warm water
1 tbsp. extra-virgin olive oil

FOR THE TOPPING:
3 tbsp. olive oil
1 large red onion, peeled and chopped
2 garlic cloves, peeled and finely sliced
1 lb. frozen spinach, thawed and drained
salt and freshly ground black pepper
3 tbsp. passata (if not available, use tomato sauce)
4 oz. mascarpone cheese
1 tbsp. toasted pine nuts

Food Fact

Traditionally, mozzarella cheese is used for pizza topping, but this recipe incorporates another Italian cheese—mascarpone—which gives a creamy-textured result to complement the delicate spinach and pine nut topping.

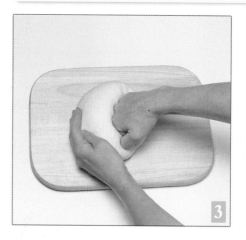

Chili Beef Calzone

1 Preheat the oven to 425° F. Heat the oil in a large saucepan and gently cook the onion and pepper for 5 minutes.

2 Add the ground beef to the saucepan, and cook for 10 minutes until browned.

3 Add the chili beans and tomatoes and simmer gently for 30 minutes or until the beef is tender. Place a cookie sheet into the preheated oven to heat up.

4 Divide the pizza dough into 4 equal pieces. Cover 3 pieces of the dough with plastic wrap and roll out the other piece on a lightly floured board to an 8-inch circle.

5 Spoon a quarter of the chili mixture onto half of the dough circle and dampen the edges with a little water.

6 Fold over the empty half of the dough and press the edges together to seal.

7 Repeat this process with the remaining dough. Place on the hot cookie sheet and bake for 15 minutes. Serve with the lettuce leaves.

INGREDIENTS
Serves 4

1 quantity pizza dough (see page 40)

1 tbsp. sunflower oil

1 onion, peeled and finely chopped

1 green bell pepper, deseeded and chopped

½ lb. ground beef

14-oz. can chili beans (precooked kidney beans in a chili sauce)

7-oz. can chopped tomatoes

mixed lettuce leaves, to serve

Tasty Tip

Calzone is a stuffed pizza which originates from Naples. For a vegetarian variation, replace the meat with sliced roasted vegetables such as bell peppers, onions, zucchini, mushrooms, and eggplant. Sprinkle some grated mozzarella cheese over the vegetables, and fold the dough over into a half-moon shape as in step 6. Serve with tomato sauce on the side.

Roquefort, Prosciutto, & Arugula Pizza

1 Preheat the oven to 425° F. Roll the pizza dough out on a lightly floured board to form a 10-inch circle.

2 Lightly cover the dough and set aside while making the sauce. Place a cookie sheet in the preheated oven to heat up.

3 Place all of the tomato sauce ingredients in a large heavy-based saucepan and slowly bring to a boil.

4 Cover and simmer for 15 minutes, uncover, and cook for an additional 10 minutes

until the sauce has thickened and reduced by half.

5 Spoon the tomato sauce over the shaped pizza dough. Place on the hot cookie sheet and bake for 10 minutes.

6 Remove the pizza from the oven and top with the Roquefort and prosciutto, then bake for an additional 10 minutes.

7 Toss the arugula in the olive oil and pile onto the pizza. Sprinkle with the Parmesan cheese and serve immediately.

Food Fact

To make a thin and crispy pizza, roll the dough out to a 12-inch circle in step 1, then continue as demonstrated. For a really crispy pizza, remove from the oven 5 minutes before the end of cooking time. Place directly under the broiler, and cook until the cheese has melted and the pizza base is crispy and golden brown.

INGREDIENTS
Serves 2–4

*1 quantity pizza dough
  (see page 40)*

BASIC TOMATO SAUCE:
2 cups canned chopped tomatoes
2 garlic cloves, peeled and crushed
grated rind of ½ lime
2 tbsp. extra-virgin olive oil
2 tbsp. freshly chopped basil
½ tsp. sugar
*salt and freshly ground black
  pepper*

FOR THE TOPPING:
*4 oz. Roquefort cheese, cut into
  chunks*
6 slices prosciutto
1 bunch arugula, rinsed
1 tbsp. extra-virgin olive oil
*8 tbsp. Parmesan cheese, freshly
  shaved*

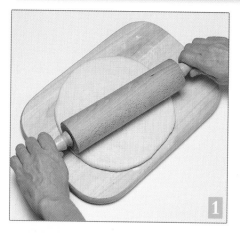

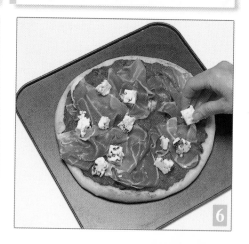

Luxury Fish Pasties

1 Preheat the oven to 400° F. Place the butter in a saucepan and slowly heat until melted.

2 Add the flour and cook, stirring for 1 minute. Remove from the heat and gradually add the milk, a little at a time, stirring between each addition.

3 Return to the heat and simmer, stirring continuously until thickened. Remove from the heat and add the salmon, parsley, dill, lime rind, lime juice, shrimp, and seasoning.

4 Roll out the pastry on a lightly floured surface and cut out 6 5-inch circles and 6 6-inch circles.

5 Brush the edges of the smaller circles with the beaten egg and place 2 tablespoons of filling in the center of each one.

6 Place the larger circle over the filling and press the edges together to seal.

7 Pinch the edge of the pastry between the forefinger and thumb to ensure a firm seal and decorative edge.

8 Cut a slit in each pastie, brush with the beaten egg, and sprinkle with sea salt.

9 Transfer to a cookie sheet, and cook in the preheated oven for 20 minutes or until golden brown. Serve immediately with some fresh green salad leaves.

INGREDIENTS
Serves 6

2 quantities quick flaky pastry (see page 20), chilled
½ cup butter
1 cup all-purpose flour
1⅓ cups milk
½ lb. salmon steak, skinned and cut into chunks
1 tbsp. freshly chopped parsley
1 tbsp. freshly chopped dill
grated rind and juice of 1 lime
½ lb. peeled shrimp
salt and freshly ground black pepper
1 small egg, beaten
1 tsp. sea salt
fresh lettuce leaves, to serve

Helpful Hint

When using raw shrimp, make sure that the vein running along the back of the shrimp is removed.

Tomato & Zucchini Herb Tart

1 Preheat the oven to 450° F. Heat 2 tablespoons of the oil in a large skillet.

2 Fry the onion and garlic for about 4 minutes until softened, and set aside.

3 Roll out the pastry on a lightly floured surface, and cut out a 12-inch circle.

4 Brush the pastry with a little beaten egg, then prick all over with a fork.

5 Transfer onto a dampened cookie sheet and bake in the preheated oven for about 10 minutes.

6 Turn the pastry over and brush with a little more egg. Bake for 5 more minutes, then remove from the oven.

7 Mix together the onion, garlic, and herbs with the goat cheese, and spread over the pastry.

8 Arrange the tomatoes and zucchini over the goat cheese, and drizzle with the remaining oil.

9 Cook for 20–25 minutes or until the pastry is golden brown and the topping is bubbling. Garnish with the thyme sprigs and serve immediately.

INGREDIENTS
Serves 4

4 tbsp. olive oil

1 onion, peeled and finely chopped

3 garlic cloves, peeled and crushed

14 oz. prepared puff pastry, thawed if frozen

1 small egg, beaten

2 tbsp. freshly chopped rosemary

2 tbsp. freshly chopped parsley

6 oz. rindless, fresh, soft goat cheese

4 ripe plum tomatoes, sliced

1 medium zucchini, trimmed and sliced

thyme sprigs, to garnish

Food Fact

Goat cheese works particularly well in this recipe, complementing both the tomatoes and zucchini. Be aware, though, that it can be a little acidic, so try to choose a creamy variety, which will mellow even more when baked.

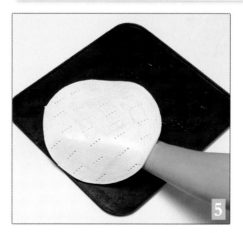

Multigrain Bread

1 Preheat the oven to 425° F. Sift the white flour and salt into a large bowl. Stir in the granary and rye flours, then rub in the butter until the mixture resembles bread crumbs. Stir in the yeast, oats, and seeds, and make a well in the center.

2 Stir the malt extract into the warm water until dissolved. Add the malt water to the dry ingredients. Mix to a soft dough.

3 Turn the dough out onto a lightly floured surface and knead for 10 minutes until smooth and elastic.

4 Put in a greased bowl, cover with plastic wrap, and leave to rise in a warm place for about 1½ hours or until the dough has doubled in size.

5 Turn out and knead again for a minute or two to eliminate the air.

6 Shape into an oval loaf, 12 inches long, and place on a well-greased baking tray.

7 Encase in greased plastic wrap and let rise for 40 minutes or until doubled in size.

8 Brush the loaf with beaten egg and bake in the preheated oven for 35–45 minutes or until the bread is well risen, browned, and sounds hollow when the base is tapped. Leave to cool on a rack, then serve.

INGREDIENTS
Makes 1 large loaf

3 cups white bread flour

2 tsp. salt

2 cups granary bread flour (if not available, use whole-wheat bread flour)

1 cup rye flour

2 tbsp. butter, diced

2 tsp. easy-blend dried yeast

⅓ cup rolled oats

2 tbsp. sunflower seeds

1 tbsp. malt extract

2 cups warm water

1 medium egg, beaten

Helpful Hint

The amount of water you need to add to the dry ingredients in this recipe will depend on the types and brands of flour you use. Add just enough water to make a soft, elastic dough.

Quick Whole-Wheat Bread

1 Preheat the oven to 400° F. Grease 2 1-lb. loaf pans. Sift the flour, salt, and sugar into a large bowl, adding the remaining bran in the sifter. Stir in the yeast, then make a well in the center.

2 Pour the warm water into the dry ingredients and mix to form a soft dough, adding a little more water if needed.

3 Knead on a lightly floured surface for 10 minutes until smooth and elastic.

4 Divide in half, shape into 2 oblong shapes, and place in the pans. Cover with greased plastic wrap and leave in a warm place for 40 minutes or until risen to the top of the pans.

5 Glaze 1 loaf with the beaten egg and dust the other loaf generously with the white flour.

6 Bake the loaves in the preheated oven for 35 minutes or until well risen and lightly browned. Turn out of the pans and return to the oven for 5 minutes to crisp the sides. Cool on a wire rack.

7 For the onion and caraway seed rolls, gently fry the onion in the oil until soft. Set aside until the onions are cool, then stir into the dry ingredients with 1 tablespoon of the caraway seeds. Make the dough as before.

8 Divide the dough into 16 pieces and shape into rolls. Put on 2 greased baking trays, cover with greased plastic wrap, and let rest for 30 minutes.

9 Glaze the rolls with milk and sprinkle with the rest of the seeds. Bake for 25–30 minutes, cool on a wire rack, and serve.

INGREDIENTS
Makes 2 1-lb. loaves

4 ¾ cups whole-wheat bread flour
2 tsp. salt
½ tsp. granulated sugar
1 tsp. easy-blend dried yeast
2 cups warm water

TO FINISH:
beaten egg, to glaze
1 tbsp. white flour, to dust

ONION & CARAWAY SEED ROLLS:
1 small onion, peeled and finely chopped
1 tbsp. olive oil
2 tbsp. caraway seeds
milk, to glaze

Helpful Hint

Typically, the bread dough is kneaded, left to rise, kneaded, shaped, and then left to rise again. This bread does not need two risings—simply knead, shape, rise, and bake.

1

4

5

Rustic Country Bread

1 Preheat the oven to 425° F. For the starter, sift the flour into a bowl. Stir in the yeast and make a well in the center. Mix in the warm water with a fork.

2 Transfer to a saucepan, cover with a clean dishtowel, and leave for 2–3 days at room temperature. Twice a day, stir the mixture and add a little water.

3 For the dough, mix the flours, salt, sugar, and yeast in a bowl. Add 1 cup of the starter, the oil, and the warm water. Mix to a soft dough.

4 Knead on a lightly floured surface for 10 minutes until smooth and elastic. Put in a greased bowl, cover, and let rise in a warm place for about 1½ hours or until doubled in size.

5 Turn the dough out and knead for a minute or two. Shape into a round loaf and place on a greased cookie sheet.

6 Cover with greased plastic wrap and leave to rise for 1 hour or until doubled in size.

7 Dust the loaf with flour, then using a sharp knife, make several cuts across the top of the loaf. Cut across the loaf in the opposite direction to make a square pattern.

8 Bake in the preheated oven for 40–45 minutes or until golden brown and hollow-sounding when tapped underneath. Cool on a wire rack and serve.

INGREDIENTS
Makes 1 large loaf

SOURDOUGH STARTER:
2 cups white bread flour
2 tsp. easy-blend dried yeast
1¼ cups warm water

BREAD DOUGH:
3 cups white bread flour
3 tbsp. rye flour
1½ tsp. salt
½ tsp. granulated sugar
1 tsp. dried yeast
1 tsp. sunflower oil
¾ cup warm water

TO FINISH:
2 tsp. all-purpose flour
2 tsp. rye flour

Helpful Hint

Put the remaining starter in a bowl, stir in ½ cup of warm water and 1 cup white bread flour. Stir twice a day for 2–3 days, and use as a starter for another loaf.

Soft Dinner Rolls

1 Preheat the oven to 425° F. Gently heat the butter, sugar, and milk in a saucepan until the butter has melted and the sugar has dissolved. Cool until tepid. Sift the flour and salt into a bowl, stir in the yeast, and make a well in the center. Set aside 1 tablespoon of the beaten eggs. Add the rest to the dry ingredients, along with the milk mixture. Mix to form a soft dough.

2 Knead the dough on a lightly floured surface for 10 minutes until smooth and elastic. Put in a greased bowl, cover with plastic wrap, and leave in a warm place to rise for 1 hour or until doubled in size. Knead again for a minute or two, then divide into 16 pieces. Shape into braids, snails, clover leaves, or cottage buns. Place on 2 greased cookie sheets, cover with greased plastic wrap, and let rise for 30 minutes until doubled in size.

3 Mix the remaining beaten egg with the milk and brush over the rolls. Sprinkle some with sea salt, others with poppy seeds, and leave some plain. Bake in the preheated oven for about 20 minutes or until golden and hollow-sounding when tapped underneath. Transfer to a wire rack. Cover with a clean dishtowel while cooling to keep the rolls soft, and serve.

INGREDIENTS
Makes 16

4 tbsp. butter
1 tbsp. granulated sugar
1 cup milk
5 cups white bread flour
1½ tsp. salt
2 tsp. easy-blend dried yeast
2 medium eggs, beaten

TO GLAZE & FINISH:
2 tbsp. milk
1 tsp. sea salt
2 tsp. poppy seeds

Helpful Hint

For braids, divide into 3 equal pieces, and roll each piece of dough into a rope about 3½ inches long. Braid, then pinch the ends together to seal. For snails, roll into a 10-inch rope, then form into a coil, tucking the end under the roll to secure.

Helpful Hint

For clover leaf rolls, divide into 3 equal pieces and roll each into a ball. Place the balls together in a triangular shape. For cottage buns, divide the dough into two-thirds and one-third pieces. Shape each piece into a flattened ball, then put the smaller one on top of the larger one. Push a floured wooden spoon handle or finger through the middle of the top one and into the bottom one to join together.

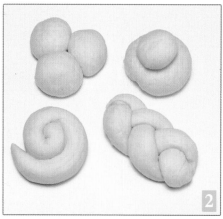

Rosemary & Olive Focaccia

1 Preheat the oven to 400° F. Sift the flour, salt, and sugar into a large bowl. Stir in the yeast and rosemary. Make a well in the center.

2 Pour in the warm water and the oil, and mix to a soft dough. Turn out onto a lightly floured surface and knead for about 10 minutes until smooth and elastic.

3 Pat the olives dry on paper towels, then gently knead into the dough. Put in a greased bowl, cover with plastic wrap, and let rise in a warm place for 1½ hours or until it has doubled in size.

4 Turn out the dough and knead again for a minute or two. Divide in half and roll out each piece to a 10-inch circle.

5 Transfer to greased cookie sheets, cover with greased plastic wrap, and allow them to rise for 30 minutes.

6 Using the fingertips, make deep dimples all over the the dough. Drizzle with the oil and sprinkle with sea salt.

7 Bake in the preheated oven for 20–25 minutes or until risen and golden. Cool on a wire rack and garnish with sprigs of rosemary.

INGREDIENTS
Makes 2 loaves

6 cups bread flour
pinch of salt
pinch of granulated sugar
1 tsp. easy-blend dried yeast
2 tsp. freshly chopped rosemary
2 cups warm water
3 tbsp. olive oil
⅓ cup pitted black olives, coarsely
  chopped
sprigs of rosemary, to garnish

TO FINISH:
3 tbsp. olive oil
coarse sea salt

Tasty Tip

As a variation, replace the rosemary with some chopped sun-dried tomatoes. Knead the tomatoes into the dough along with the olives in step 3, then before baking, drizzle with the oil and replace the salt with some grated mozzarella cheese.

Daktyla-Style Bread

1 Preheat the oven to 425° F. Sift the flours and salt into a large bowl, adding the bran left in the sifter. Stir in the cornmeal and yeast. Make a well in the center.

2 Put the honey, oil, milk, and water in a saucepan, and heat gently until tepid. Add to the dry ingredients and mix to a soft dough, adding a little more water if needed.

3 Knead the dough on a lightly floured surface for 10 minutes until smooth and elastic. Put in a greased bowl, cover with plastic wrap, and let rise in a warm place for about 1½ hours or until it has doubled in size.

4 Turn the dough out and knead for a minute or two. Shape into a long oval about 10 inches long. Cut the oval into 6 equal pieces. Shape each piece into an oblong, then arrange in a row on a greased cookie sheet so that all the pieces of dough are touching.

5 Cover with greased plastic wrap and leave for 45 minutes or until doubled in size.

6 Brush the bread with milk, then top with sesame seeds.

7 Bake the bread in the preheated oven for 40–45 minutes or until golden brown and hollow-sounding when tapped underneath. Cool on a rack and serve.

INGREDIENTS
Makes 1 loaf

3 cups white bread flour
1 cup whole-wheat flour
1 tsp. salt
1 cup fine cornmeal
2 tsp. easy-blend dried yeast
2 tsp. honey
1 tbsp. olive oil
4 tbsp. milk
1 cup plus 1 tbsp. water

TO GLAZE & FINISH:
4 tbsp. milk
4 tbsp. sesame seeds

Food Fact

Daktyla was traditionally made in Cyprus during Lent. The Cypriots made crisp, syrup-soaked fingers of pastry filled with an almond-and-cinnamon filling. In this recipe, the bread is shaped into oblongs and baked so that the bread can be broken into pieces to eat.

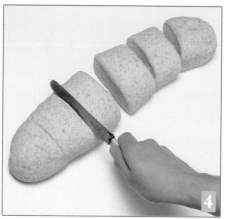

Spiced Apple Doughnuts

1 Sift the flour, salt, and 1 teaspoon of the cinnamon into a large bowl. Stir in the yeast and make a well in the center.

2 Add the milk, butter, and egg, and mix to a soft dough. Knead on a lightly floured surface for 10 minutes until smooth and elastic.

3 Divide the dough into 8 pieces and shape each into a ball. Put on a floured cookie sheet, cover with greased plastic wrap, and leave in a warm place for about 1 hour or until doubled in size.

4 To make the filling, put the apples in a saucepan with the sugar, lemon juice, and 3 tablespoons of water. Cover and simmer for about 10 minutes, then uncover and cook until fairly dry, stirring occasionally. Mash, or blend in a food processor to a purée.

5 Pour enough oil into a deep fryer to come one-third of the way up the pan. Heat the oil to 350° F, then deep-fry the doughnuts for 1½–2 minutes on each side until well browned.

6 Drain the doughnuts on paper towels, and roll in the sugar mixed with the rest of the cinnamon. Push a thick skewer into the center to make a hole and pipe in the filling. Serve warm or cold.

INGREDIENTS
Makes 8

2 cups flour
½ tsp. salt
1½ tsp. ground cinnamon
1 tsp. easy-blend dried yeast
6 tbsp. warm milk
2 tbsp. butter, melted
1 medium egg, beaten
oil, to deep fry
4 tbsp. granulated sugar, to coat

FOR THE FILLING:

2 small apples, peeled, cored, and
  chopped
2 tsp. light brown sugar
2 tsp. lemon juice

Tasty Tip

These doughnuts are also excellent when filled with pears. Simply replace the 2 apples with 2 pears and continue with the recipe. Look for Comice pears, as they are considered to be among the best on the market. When choosing pears, select those that are fragrant and free of blemishes.

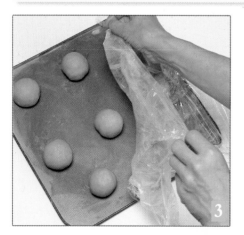

3

5

6

Bacon & Tomato Breakfast Twist

1 Preheat the oven to 400° F. Sift the flour and salt into a large bowl. Stir in the yeast and make a well in the center. Pour in the milk and butter, and mix to a soft dough.

2 Knead on a lightly floured surface for 10 minutes until smooth and elastic. Put in a greased bowl, cover with plastic wrap, and let rise in a warm place for 1 hour until doubled in size.

3 Cook the bacon under a hot broiler for 5–6 minutes or until crisp, turning once. Allow the bacon to cool, then chop.

4 Knead the dough again for a minute or two. Roll it out to a 10 x 13 inch rectangle. Cut in half lengthwise. Lightly brush with butter, then sprinkle with the bacon, tomatoes, and black pepper, leaving a ½-inch margin around the edges.

5 Brush the edges of the dough with beaten egg, then roll up each rectangle lengthwise.

6 Place the 2 rolls side-by-side and twist together, pinching the ends to seal.

7 Transfer to a greased cookie sheet, and cover loosely with greased plastic wrap. Let rise in a warm place for about 30 minutes.

8 Brush with the beaten egg and sprinkle with the oatmeal. Bake in the preheated oven for about 30 minutes or until golden brown and hollow-sounding when tapped on the base. Serve the bread warm in thick slices.

INGREDIENTS
Serves 8

4 cups bread flour
½ tsp. salt
1 tsp. easy-blend dried yeast
1¼ cups warm milk
1 tbsp. butter, melted

FOR THE FILLING:
½ lb. bacon
1 tbsp. butter, melted
1 medium, ripe tomato, peeled,
  deseeded, and chopped
freshly ground black pepper

TO FINISH:
beaten egg, to glaze
2 tsp. quick oats

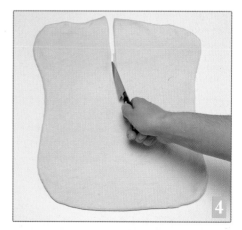

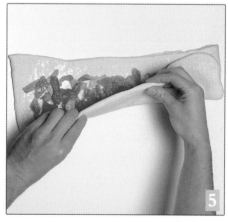

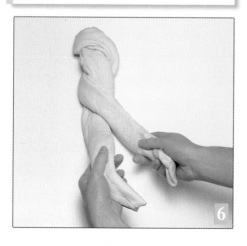

Cheese-Crusted Potato Scones

1 Preheat the oven to 425° F. Sift the flours, salt, and baking powder into a large bowl. Rub in the butter until the mixture resembles fine bread crumbs.

2 Stir 4 tablespoons of the milk into the mashed potatoes, and season with black pepper.

3 Add the dry ingredients to the potato mixture, mixing together with a fork, and add the remaining 1 tablespoon of milk if needed.

4 Knead the dough on a lightly floured surface for a few seconds until smooth. Roll out to a 6-inch circle, and transfer to a greased cookie sheet.

5 Mark the scone circle into 6 wedges, cutting about halfway through with a small, sharp knife.

6 Brush with milk, then sprinkle with the cheese and a light dusting of paprika.

7 Bake on the center shelf of the preheated oven for 15 minutes or until well risen and golden brown.

8 Transfer to a wire rack and let cool for 5 minutes before breaking into wedges.

9 Serve warm, or let cool completely. Once cool, store the scones in an airtight container. Garnish with a sprig of basil and serve split and buttered.

INGREDIENTS
Makes 6

1½ cups plus 3 tbsp. self-rising flour
3 tbsp. whole-wheat flour
½ tsp. salt
1½ tsp. baking powder
2 tbsp. butter, cubed
5 tbsp. milk
¾ cup cold mashed potatoes
freshly ground black pepper

TO FINISH:

2 tbsp. milk
6 tbsp. cheddar cheese, finely grated
paprika, to dust
basil leaves, to garnish

Food Fact

The scone supposedly acquired its name from the Stone of Destiny (or "Scone") in Scotland, where Scottish Kings were once crowned.

Moist Mincemeat Tea Loaf

1 Preheat the oven to 350° F. Grease and line the base of a 2-lb. loaf pan with nonstick baking parchment.

2 Sift the flour and mixed spice into a large bowl. Add the butter and rub in until the mixture resembles bread crumbs.

3 Put aside 2 tablespoons of the slivered almonds, and stir in the rest with the candied cherries and sugar.

4 Make a well in the center of the dry ingredients. Lightly beat the eggs, then stir in the mincemeat, lemon zest, and brandy or milk.

5 Add the egg mixture and fold together until blended. Spoon into the prepared loaf pan, smooth the top with the back of a spoon, then sprinkle over the remaining slivered almonds.

6 Bake on the center shelf of the preheated oven for 30 minutes. Cover with foil to prevent the almonds from browning too much. Bake for an additional 30 minutes or until well risen and a skewer inserted into the center comes out clean.

7 Leave the tea loaf in the pan for 10 minutes before removing and cooling on a wire rack. Remove the lining paper, slice thickly, and serve.

INGREDIENTS
Cuts into 12 slices

2 cups self-rising flour
½ tsp. ground mixed spice
½ cup cold butter, cubed
¾ cup slivered almonds
¼ cup candied cherries, rinsed, dried, and quartered
⅓ cup brown sugar
2 medium eggs
2 cups prepared mincemeat
1 tsp. lemon zest
2 tsp. brandy or milk

Food Fact

Traditionally, mincemeat contained cooked lean beef, but it is often omitted today. Mincemeat is now part of Thanksgiving and Christmas fare in the United States.

Marbled Chocolate & Orange Loaf

1 Preheat the oven to 350° F. Lightly grease a 1-lb. loaf pan and line the base with a layer of nonstick baking parchment.

2 Put the chocolate in a bowl set over a saucepan of very hot water. Stir occasionally until melted. Remove, and leave until just cool but not starting to harden.

3 Meanwhile, cream together the butter, sugar, and orange zest until pale and fluffy. Gradually add the beaten eggs, beating well after each addition.

4 Sift in the flour, add the orange juice, and fold with a metal spoon or rubber spatula. Divide the mixture into 2 separate bowls. Gently fold the cocoa and chocolate into 1 bowl of the mixture.

5 Drop tablespoonfuls of each cake mixture into the prepared pan, alternating between the orange and chocolate mixtures. Briefly swirl the colors together with a knife to give a marbled effect.

6 Bake in the preheated oven for 40 minutes or until firm and a fine skewer inserted into the center comes out clean. Leave in the pan for 5 minutes, then turn out, and cool on a wire rack. Carefully remove the baking parchment.

7 Dust the cake with the confectioners' sugar and then with the cocoa. Cut into thick slices and serve.

INGREDIENTS
Cuts into 6 slices

⅓ cup semisweet chocolate chips
½ cup butter, softened
½ cup granulated sugar
zest of 1 orange
2 medium eggs, beaten
1 cup self-rising flour
2 tsp. orange juice
1 tbsp. unsweetened cocoa, sifted

TO FINISH:
1 tbsp. confectioners' sugar
1 tsp. cocoa powder

Tasty Tip

To make a cream cheese frosting, beat together 6 tablespoons of cream cheese with 1–2 tablespoons of milk until smooth. Add a pinch of salt, 1 teaspoon of vanilla extract, and 2 cups of confectioners' sugar, and mix well. Spread on top of the cake when cool.

Fruity Apple Tea Bread

1 Preheat the oven to 350° F. Grease and line the base of a 2-lb. loaf pan with nonstick baking parchment.

2 Put the butter, sugar, golden raisins, and apple juice in a small saucepan. Heat gently, stirring occasionally, until the butter has melted. Pour into a bowl and allow it to cool.

3 Stir in the chopped apple and beaten eggs. Sift the flour, spices, and baking soda over the apple mixture.

4 Mix together, spoon into the prepared loaf pan, and smooth the top with the back of a spoon.

5 Toss the apple slices in lemon juice and arrange on top.

6 Bake in the preheated oven for 50 minutes. Cover with foil to prevent the top from browning too much.

7 Bake for 30–35 minutes or until a skewer inserted into the center comes out clean.

8 Leave in the pan for 10 minutes, then turn out onto a wire rack to cool.

9 Brush the top with corn syrup and let cool. Remove the baking parchment, cut into thick slices, and serve with curls of butter.

INGREDIENTS
Cuts into 12 slices

½ cup butter
½ cup golden brown sugar
2 cups golden raisins
⅔ cup apple juice
1 apple, peeled cored, and chopped
2 medium eggs, beaten
2½ cups all-purpose flour
½ tsp. ground cinnamon
½ tsp. ground ginger
2 tsp. baking soda
curls of butter, to serve

TO DECORATE:
1 apple, cored and sliced
1 tsp. lemon juice
1 tbsp. light corn syrup, warmed

Tasty Tip

For a variation of this cake, soak the golden raisins in brandy overnight before adding them in step 2. To make the tea bread moister in texture, add 1 grated carrot at the same time as the chopped apple in step 3.

Baked Lemon & Golden Raisin Cheesecake

1 Preheat the oven to 325° F. Grease an 8-inch springform cake pan with nonstick baking parchment.

2 Beat 4 tablespoons of the sugar and the butter together until light and creamy, then stir in the self-rising flour, baking powder, and 1 egg.

3 Mix lightly together until well blended. Spoon into the prepared pan and spread the mixture over the base. Separate the 4 remaining eggs and set aside.

4 Blend the cheese in a food processor until soft. Gradually add the eggs yolks and sugar, and blend until smooth. Turn into a bowl and stir in the rest of the flour, lemon rind, and juice.

5 Mix lightly before adding the crème fraîche and golden raisins, stirring well.

6 Beat the egg whites until stiff, fold into the cheese mixture, and pour into the pan. Tap lightly on the surface to remove any air bubbles. Bake in the preheated oven for about 1 hour or until golden and firm.

7 Cover lightly if browning too much. Turn the oven off and leave in the oven to cool for 2–3 hours.

8 Remove the cheesecake from the oven and, when completely cold, remove from the pan. Sprinkle with the confectioners' sugar, decorate with the blueberries and mint leaves, and serve.

INGREDIENTS
Cuts into 10 slices

1¼ cups granulated sugar
4 tbsp. butter
½ cup self-rising flour
½ tsp. baking powder
5 large eggs
2 cups cream cheese
4 tbsp. all-purpose flour
grated rind of 1 lemon
3 tbsp. fresh lemon juice
½ cup crème fraîche
½ cup golden raisins

TO DECORATE:
1 tbsp. confectioners' sugar
fresh blueberries
mint leaves

Tasty Tip

Vary the flavor by adding a little freshly grated nutmeg and ½ teaspoon of ground cinnamon to the base in step 2. Add a little of both spices to the confectioners' sugar before sprinkling.

Crunchy Rhubarb Crumble

1 Preheat the oven to 350° F. Place the flour in a large bowl and cut the butter into cubes. Add to the flour and rub in with your fingertips until the mixture looks like fine bread crumbs, or blend for a few seconds in a food processor.

2 Stir in the rolled oats, brown sugar, sesame seeds, and cinnamon. Mix well and set aside.

3 Prepare the rhubarb by removing the thick ends of the stems and cut diagonally into 1-inch chunks. Wash thoroughly under cold running water and pat dry with a clean dishtowel. Place the rhubarb in a 1-quart casserole dish.

4 Sprinkle the sugar over the rhubarb and top with the crumble mixture. Level the top of the crumble so that all the fruit is well covered, and press down firmly. If desired, sprinkle a little extra granulated sugar on the top..

5 Place on a cookie sheet and bake in the preheated oven for 40–50 minutes or until the fruit is soft and the topping is golden brown. Sprinkle the pudding with some more granulated sugar and serve hot with custard sauce or cream.

INGREDIENTS
Serves 6

1 cup all-purpose flour
4 tbsp. softened butter
⅔ cup rolled oats
4 tbsp. brown sugar
1 tbsp. sesame seeds
½ tsp. ground cinnamon
1 lb. fresh rhubarb
4 tbsp. granulated sugar
custard sauce or cream, to serve

Tasty Tip
To make homemade custard, pour 2½ cups of milk with a few drops of vanilla extract into a saucepan and bring to a boil. Remove from the heat and let cool. Meanwhile, beat 5 egg yolks and 3 tablespoons of granulated sugar together in a mixing bowl until thick and pale in color. Add the milk, stir, and strain into a heavy-based saucepan. Cook on a low heat, stirring constantly until the consistency of heavy cream. Pour over the rhubarb crumble and serve.

Iced Bakewell Tart

1 Preheat the oven to 400° F. Place the flour and salt in a bowl, and rub in the butter and shortening until the mixture resembles bread crumbs. Alternatively, blend quickly, in short bursts, in a food processor.

2 Add the eggs with enough water to make a soft, pliable dough. Knead lightly on a floured board, then chill in the refrigerator for about 30 minutes. Roll out the pastry and use to line a 9-inch, loose-bottomed tart pan.

3 For the filling, mix together the melted butter, sugar, almonds, and beaten eggs, and add a few drops of almond extract. Spread the base of the pastry shell with the raspberry jam and spoon over the egg mixture.

4 Bake in the preheated oven for about 30 minutes or until the filling is firm and golden brown. Remove from the oven and let cool completely.

5 When the tart is cold, make the frosting by mixing together the confectioners' sugar and lemon juice, a little at a time, until the frosting is smooth and of a spreadable consistency.

6 Spread the frosting over the tart, leave to set for 2–3 minutes, and sprinkle with the almonds. Chill in the refrigerator for about 10 minutes, and serve.

INGREDIENTS
Cuts into 8 slices

FOR THE RICH PASTRY:
1½ cups all-purpose flour
pinch of salt
5 tbsp. butter, cut into small pieces
4 tbsp. shortening, cut into small pieces
2 small egg yolks, beaten

FOR THE FILLING:
½ cup butter, melted
½ cup granulated sugar
1 cup ground almonds
2 large eggs, beaten
few drops of almond extract
2 tbsp. raspberry jelly

FOR THE ICING:
1 cup confectioners' sugar, sifted
6–8 tsp. fresh lemon juice
¼ cup toasted, slivered almonds

Tasty Tip

This tart is delicious when served with spoonfuls of thick plain yogurt or traditional vanilla ice cream. It is not essential to use raspberry jelly in this recipe. If you don't have raspberry jelly handy, use any seedless jelly available. Blackberry jelly would work particularly well.

Apricot & Almond Slice

1 Preheat the oven to 350° F. Grease an 8-inch square pan and line with nonstick baking parchment.

2 Sprinkle the brown sugar and the slivered almonds over the baking parchment, then arrange the apricot halves cut-side down on top.

3 Cream the butter and sugar together in a large bowl until light and fluffy.

4 Gradually beat the eggs into the butter mixture, adding a spoonful of flour after each addition of egg.

5 When all the eggs have been added, stir in the remaining flour and ground almonds, and mix thoroughly.

6 Add the almond extract and the apricots, and stir well.

7 Spoon the mixture into the prepared pan, taking care not to dislodge the apricot halves. Bake in the preheated oven for 1 hour or until golden and firm to touch.

8 Remove from the oven and let cool slightly for 15–20 minutes. Turn out carefully, discard the baking parchment, and transfer to a serving dish. Pour the honey over the top of the cake, sprinkle with the toasted almonds, and serve.

INGREDIENTS
Cuts into 10 slices

2 tbsp. brown sugar

¼ cup slivered almonds

14-oz. can apricot halves, drained

1 cup butter

1 cup granulated sugar

4 medium eggs

1½ cups plus 3 tbsp. self-rising flour

¼ cup ground almonds

½ tsp. almond extract

⅓ cup dried apricots, chopped

3 tbsp. honey

3 tbsp. coarsely chopped almonds, toasted

Helpful Hint

This cake should keep for about three to five days if stored correctly. Let the cake cool completely, then remove from the pan and discard the lining paper. Store in an airtight container lined with waxed paper or baking parchment, and keep in a cool place.

Queen of Puddings

1 Preheat the oven to 325° F. Grease a 1-quart ovenproof baking dish.

2 Mix the bread crumbs and sugar together in a bowl.

3 Pour the milk into a small saucepan and heat gently with the butter and lemon rind until the butter has melted.

4 Let the mixture cool a little, then pour in the bread crumbs. Stir well and let soak for 30 minutes.

5 Beat the egg yolks into the cooled bread-crumb mixture and pour into the prepared dish.

6 Place the dish on a cookie sheet and bake in the preheated oven for about 30 minutes or until firm and set. Remove from the oven.

7 Let cool slightly, then spread the jelly over the pudding. Beat the egg whites until stiff and standing in peaks.

8 Gently fold in the granulated sugar with a metal spoon or rubber spatula. Pile the meringue over the top.

9 Return the dish to the oven for an additional 25–30 minutes or until the meringue is crisp and just slightly browned. Serve hot or cold.

INGREDIENTS
Serves 4

1½ cups fresh white bread crumbs
2 tbsp. granulated sugar
2 cups whole milk
2 tbsp. butter
grated rind of 1 small lemon
2 medium eggs, separated
2 tbsp. raspberry jelly
4 tbsp. granulated sugar

Helpful Hint

When beating egg whites, it is imperative that the bowl is completely clean and free of any grease. To make sure that the meringue does not collapse, beat the egg whites until stiff. Gradually add the sugar, a spoonful at a time, beating well between each addition. Place in the oven immediately after all of the sugar has been added.

Eve's Pudding

1 Preheat the oven to 350° F. Grease a 1-quart casserole dish.

2 Peel, core, and slice the apples, and place a layer in the base of the prepared dish.

3 Sprinkle a little brown sugar and lemon rind over some of the blackberries.

4 Layer the apple and blackberries in this way until all the ingredients have been used.

5 Cream the sugar and butter together until light and fluffy.

6 Beat in the vanilla extract and then the eggs, a little at a time, adding a spoonful of flour after each addition. Fold in the extra flour with a metal spoon or rubber spatula and mix well.

7 Spread the sponge mixture over the top of the fruit and level with the back of a spoon.

8 Place the dish on a cookie sheet and bake in the preheated oven for 35–40 minutes or until well risen and golden brown. To test if the pudding is cooked, press the cooked sponge cake lightly with a clean finger—if it springs back, the sponge is cooked.

9 Dust the pudding with a little confectioners' sugar and serve immediately with the custard or cream.

INGREDIENTS
Serves 6

1 lb. apples
1 generous cup blackberries
6 tbsp. brown sugar
grated rind of 1 lemon
½ cup granulated sugar
½ cup butter
few drops of vanilla extract
2 medium eggs, beaten
1 cup self-rising flour
1 tbsp. confectioners' sugar
custard sauce or cream, to serve

Food Fact

Eve's pudding is a classic English pudding and has been popular since the early 20th century. At that time, there were many different varieties of apples grown throughout England. Unfortunately, many of these apples have now disappeared.

Lemon & Apricot Pudding

1 Preheat the oven to 350° F. Grease a 1-quart casserole dish.

2 Soak the apricots in the orange juice for 10–15 minutes or until most of the juice has been absorbed, then place in the base of the casserole.

3 Cream the butter and sugar together with the lemon rind until light and fluffy.

4 Separate the eggs. Beat the egg yolks into the creamed mixture with a spoonful of flour after each addition. Add the remaining flour, and beat well until smooth.

5 Stir the milk and lemon juice into the creamed mixture. Beat the egg whites in a clean mixing bowl until stiff and standing in peaks. Fold into the mixture using a metal spoon or rubber spatula.

6 Pour into the prepared dish and place in a roasting pan filled with enough cold water to come halfway up the sides of the dish.

7 Bake in the preheated oven for about 45 minutes or until the sponge is firm and golden brown. Remove from the oven. Serve immediately with the custard sauce or fresh cream.

INGREDIENTS
Serves 4

1 scant cup dried apricots
3 tbsp. orange juice, warmed
4 tbsp. butter
½ cup granulated sugar
juice and grated rind of 2 lemons
2 medium eggs
½ cup self-rising flour
1¼ cups milk
custard or fresh cream, to serve

Helpful Hint

This pudding is cooked in a bain-marie to control the temperature around the dish—it needs to stay at just below boiling point. Bain-maries are ideal when cooking custards, sauces, and other egg dishes. When using one, make sure that the water is kept at a constant level.

Strawberry Flan

1 Preheat the oven to 400° F. Place the flour, butter, and shortening in a food processor and blend until the mixture resembles fine bread crumbs. Stir in the sugar, then, with the machine running, add the egg yolk and enough water to make a stiff dough. Knead lightly, cover, and chill in the refrigerator for 30 minutes.

2 Roll out the pastry and use to line a 9-inch, loose-bottomed tart pan. Place a piece of waxed paper in the pastry shell, and cover with baking beans. Bake in the preheated oven for 15–20 minutes until just firm. Set aside until cool.

3 Make the filling by beating the eggs and sugar together until thick and pale. Gradually stir in the flour and then the milk. Pour into a small saucepan, and simmer for 3–4 minutes, stirring throughout.

4 Add the vanilla extract to taste, then pour into a bowl and let cool. Cover with waxed paper to prevent a skin from forming.

5 When the filling is cold, beat until smooth, then pour onto the cooked flan shell. Slice the strawberries and arrange on the top of the filling. Decorate with the mint leaves and serve.

INGREDIENTS
Serves 6

SWEET PASTRY:
1½ cups all-purpose flour
4 tbsp. butter
4 tbsp. shortening
2 tsp. granulated sugar
1 medium egg yolk, beaten

FOR THE FILLING:
1 medium egg, plus 1 extra egg yolk
4 tbsp. granulated sugar
3 tbsp. all-purpose flour
2½ cups milk
few drops of vanilla extract
3 cups strawberries, cleaned and hulled
mint leaves, to decorate

Tasty Tip

In the summer, when the choice of fruit is greater, why not try topping the flan with a variety of mixed fruits? Arrange strawberries, raspberries, kiwi fruit, and blueberries on top of the filling. If desired, heat 3 tablespoons of raspberry jelly with 2 teaspoons of lemon juice. Stir until smooth, then use to brush over the fruit. Allow it to set before serving.

Rich Double-Crust Plum Pie

1 Preheat the oven to 400° F. Make the pastry by rubbing the butter and shortening into the flour until it resembles fine bread crumbs, or blend in a food processor. Add the egg yolks and enough water to make a soft dough. Knead lightly, then wrap, and leave in the refrigerator for about 30 minutes.

2 Meanwhile, prepare the fruit. Rinse and dry the plums, then cut in half and remove the pits. Slice the plums into chunks, and cook in a saucepan with 2 tablespoons of the sugar and 2 tablespoons of water for 5–7 minutes or until slightly softened. Remove from the heat and add the remaining sugar to taste and let cool.

3 Roll out half the chilled dough on a lightly floured surface and use to line the base and sides of a 1-quart casserole

dish. Let the dough hang over the edge of the dish. Spoon in the prepared plums.

4 Roll out the remaining dough to use as the lid, and brush the edge with some water. Wrap the dough around the rolling pin and place over the plums.

5 Press the edges together to seal, and mark a decorative edge around the rim of the pastry by pinching with the thumb and forefinger or using the back of a fork.

6 Brush the lid with milk, and make a few slits in the top. Use any trimmings to decorate the top. Place on a cookie sheet and bake in the preheated oven for 30 minutes or until golden. Sprinkle with a little granulated sugar and serve hot or cold.

INGREDIENTS
Serves 6

FOR THE PASTRY:
6 tbsp. butter
6 tbsp. shortening
2 cups all-purpose flour
2 medium egg yolks

FOR THE FILLING:
1 lb. fresh plums
4 tbsp. granulated sugar
1 tbsp. milk
a little extra granulated sugar

Helpful Hint

Fresh plums are available from May to late October. When choosing plums, look for ones that are firm and give slightly to pressure. Avoid those with cracks, soft spots, or brown discolorations.

Baked Apple Dumplings

1 Preheat the oven to 400° F. Lightly grease a baking tray. Place the flour and salt in a large bowl and stir in the suet.

2 Add just enough water to the mixture to make a soft, but not sticky, dough, using your fingertips.

3 Turn the dough onto a lightly floured board and knead lightly into a ball.

4 Divide the dough into 4 pieces and roll out each piece into a thin square, large enough to encase the apples.

5 Peel and core the apples and place 1 apple in the center of each square of pastry.

6 Fill the center of the apple with mincemeat, brush the edges of each pastry square with water, and draw the corners up to meet over each apple.

7 Press the edges of the pastry firmly together, and decorate with pastry leaves and shapes made from the extra pastry trimmings.

8 Place the apples on the prepared baking tray, brush with the egg white, and sprinkle with the sugar.

9 Bake in the preheated oven for 30 minutes or until golden and the pastry and apples are cooked. Serve the apple dumplings hot with the custard or vanilla sauce.

INGREDIENTS
Serves 4

2 cups self-rising flour
¼ tsp. salt
½ cup shredded suet
4 medium apples
4–6 tsp. mincemeat
1 medium egg white, beaten
2 tsp. granulated sugar
custard or vanilla sauce, to serve

Tasty Tip

To make vanilla sauce, blend 1½ tablespoons of cornstarch with 3 tablespoons of milk to a smooth paste. Bring just under 1¼ cups of milk to just below boiling point. Stir in the cornstarch paste and cook over a gentle heat, stirring throughout until thickened and smooth. Remove from the heat and add 1 tablespoon of granulated sugar, a pat of butter, and ½ teaspoon of vanilla extract. Stir until the sugar and butter have melted, then serve.

Tasty Tip

For a homemade mincemeat, mix together ⅔ cup of mixed fruit and 1 tablespoon of toasted slivered almonds. Add 2 tablespoons of butter, 2 tablespoons of light brown sugar, and 1 teaspoon of mixed spices. Warm on a low heat, stirring. Place a spoonful into the center of the apple and continue with the recipe.

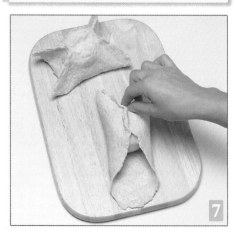

Jam Roly-poly

1 Preheat the oven to 400° F. Make the pastry by sifting the flour and salt into a large bowl.

2 Add the suet and mix lightly, then add the water, a little at a time, and mix to form a soft and pliable dough. Take care not to make the dough too wet.

3 Turn the dough out onto a lightly floured board and knead gently until smooth.

4 Roll the dough out into a 9 x 11 inch rectangle.

5 Spread the jelly over the pastry, leaving a border of ½ inch all around. Fold the border over the jam and brush the edges with water.

6 Lightly roll up the rectangle from one of the short sides, seal the top edge, and press the ends together. Do not roll the pudding up too tightly.

7 Turn the pudding upside-down onto a large piece of waxed paper large enough to come halfway up the sides. If using nonstick paper, then grease lightly.

8 Fasten the ends of the paper to make a boat-shaped paper case for the pudding to sit in, and to leave room for the roly-poly to expand.

9 Brush the pudding lightly with milk and sprinkle with the sugar. Bake in the preheated oven for 30–40 minutes or until well risen and golden. Serve immediately with the jelly sauce.

INGREDIENTS
Serves 6

2 cups self-rising flour
¼ tsp. salt
½ cup shredded suet
⅔ cup water
3 tbsp. strawberry jelly
1 tbsp. milk, to glaze
1 tsp. granulated sugar
jelly sauce, to serve

Tasty Tip

To make jelly sauce, warm 4 tablespoons of jelly, for example, raspberry jelly, with ¼ cup of water or orange juice. Stir until smooth. Blend 2 teaspoons of arrowroot with 1 tablespoon of water or juice to a smooth paste. Bring the mixture to almost boiling, then stir in the blended arrowroot. Cook, stirring, until the mixture thickens slightly and clears, then serve with the Jam Roly-poly.

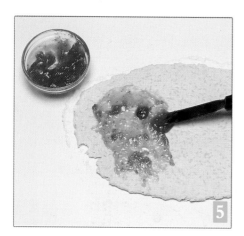

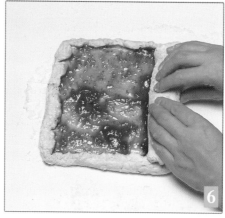

College Pudding

1 Preheat the oven to 350° F. Lightly grease an ovenproof casserole dish and place a small circle of baking parchment in the base.

2 Mix the shredded suet and bread crumbs together, and rub lightly together with the fingertips to remove any large lumps.

3 Stir in the dried fruit, spices, sugar, and baking powder. Add the eggs, and beat lightly together until the mixture is well blended and the fruit is evenly distributed.

4 Spoon the mixture into the prepared pudding basin and level the surface. Place on a baking tray and cover lightly with waxed paper.

5 Bake in the preheated oven for 20 minutes, then remove the paper and continue to bake for an additional 10–15 minutes or until the top is firm.

6 When the pudding is cooked, remove from the oven and carefully turn out onto a warmed serving dish. Decorate with the orange zest and serve immediately.

INGREDIENTS
Serves 4

½ cup shredded suet
2 cups fresh white bread crumbs
⅓ cup golden raisins
⅓ cup seedless raisins
½ tsp. ground cinnamon
¼ tsp. freshly grated nutmeg
¼ tsp. mixed spice
4 tbsp. granulated sugar
½ tsp. baking powder
2 medium eggs, beaten
orange zest, to garnish

Tasty Tip

Like many other suet puddings, this recipe is relatively cheap to make. For extra fruitiness, add some apple sauce to the mixture. To make applesauce, peel, core, and chop 1 cooking apple. Place in a saucepan with 2 tablespoons of sugar and 4 tablespoons of water. Simmer until softened but not falling apart, then roughly mash. Add the applesauce to the mixture in step 3 and continue as before.

Cherry Batter Pudding

1 Preheat the oven to 425° F. Lightly grease a shallow casserole dish.

2 Rinse the cherries, drain well, and remove the pits (using a cherry pitter if possible). If using canned cherries, drain well, discard the juice, and place in the prepared dish.

3 Sift the flour and salt into a large bowl. Stir in 2 tablespoons of the granulated sugar, and make a well in the center. Beat the eggs, then pour into the well of the dry ingredients.

4 Warm the milk, and slowly pour into the well, beating throughout and gradually drawing in the flour from the sides of the bowl. Continue until a smooth batter has formed.

5 Melt the butter in a small saucepan over a low heat, then stir into the batter with the rum. Put aside for 15 minutes, then beat again until smooth and easy to pour.

6 Pour into the prepared baking dish, and bake in the preheated oven for 30–35 minutes or until golden brown and set.

7 Remove the pudding from the oven, sprinkle with the remaining sugar, and serve hot with plenty of heavy cream.

INGREDIENTS
Serves 4

1 lb. fresh cherries (or 16-oz. can pitted cherries)
6 tbsp. all-purpose flour
pinch of salt
3 tbsp. granulated sugar
2 medium eggs
1¼ cups milk
3 tbsp. butter
1 tbsp. rum
extra granulated sugar, to dust
heavy cream, to serve

Food Fact

The traditional name of this French speciality is *clafoutis*. For that extra hit of cherry flavor, why not replace the rum used in this recipe with *kirsch*—an eau-de-vie rather than a liquor, which is made from pine nuts and cherry juice to produce a brandy. It is made in Alsace as well as in the Black Forest region in Germany.

Lemon & Ginger Buns

1 Preheat the oven to 425° F. Cut the butter or margarine into small pieces and place in a large bowl.

2 Sift the flour, baking powder, ginger, and salt together, and add to the butter, along with the lemon rind.

3 Using your fingertips, rub the butter into the flour-and-spice mixture until it resembles coarse bread crumbs.

4 Stir in the sugar, golden raisins, chopped candied peel, and stem ginger.

5 Add the egg and lemon juice to the mixture, then using a round bladed knife, stir well to mix. (The mixture should be quite stiff and just holding together.)

6 Place heaping tablespoons of the mixture onto a lightly greased baking tray, making sure that the dollops of mixture are well apart.

7 Using a fork, roughen the edges of the buns and bake in the preheated oven for 12–15 minutes.

8 Leave the buns to cool for 5 minutes before transferring to a wire rack. Let stand until cooled, then serve. Otherwise, store the buns in an airtight container and eat within 3–5 days.

INGREDIENTS
Makes 15

½ cup butter or margarine
3 cups all-purpose flour
2 tsp. baking powder
½ tsp. ground ginger
pinch of salt
finely grated rind of 1 lemon
1 cup golden brown sugar
⅔ cup golden raisins
½ cup chopped candied peel
2 tbsp. stem ginger, finely chopped
1 medium egg
juice of 1 lemon

Tasty Tip

For a gooey, sticky treat, brush the buns with a little syrup from the jar of stem ginger and sprinkle with some finely chopped stem ginger as soon as they have been removed from the oven.

Apple & Cinnamon Crumb Cake

1 Preheat the oven to 350 °F. Lightly grease and line the base of an 8-inch round cake pan with waxed paper or baking parchment.

2 Finely chop the apples and mix with the lemon juice. Set aside while making the cake.

3 For the crumble topping, sift the flour and cinnamon together into a large bowl.

4 Rub the butter or margarine into the flour and cinnamon until the mixture resembles coarse bread crumbs.

5 Stir the brown sugar into the bread crumbs and set aside.

6 For the base, cream the butter or margarine and sugar together until light and fluffy. Gradually beat the eggs into the sugar-and-butter mixture a little at a time until all the egg has been added.

7 Sift the flour, and gently fold in with a metal spoon or rubber spatula.

8 Spoon into the base of the prepared cake pan. Arrange the apple pieces on top, then lightly stir the milk into the crumble mixture.

9 Sprinkle the crumble over the apples, and bake in the preheated oven for 1½ hours. Serve cold with cream or custard sauce.

INGREDIENTS
Cuts into 8 slices

FOR THE TOPPING:
¾ lb. apples, peeled
1 tbsp. lemon juice
1 cup self-rising flour
1 tsp. ground cinnamon
6 tbsp. butter or margarine
6 tbsp. brown sugar
1 tbsp. milk

FOR THE BASE:
½ cup butter or margarine
4 tbsp. granulated sugar
2 medium eggs
1 cup plus 3 tbsp. self-rising flour
cream or freshly made custard sauce, to serve

Tasty Tip
For a crunchier-textured topping, stir in ½ cup of chopped mixed nuts and seeds to the crumble mixture in step 5.

Chocolate & Coconut Cake

1 Preheat the oven to 350° F. Melt the chocolate in a small bowl placed over a saucepan of gently simmering water, making sure that the base of the bowl does not touch the water. When the chocolate has melted, stir until smooth and let cool.

2 Lightly grease and line the bases of 2 7-inch round cake pans with baking parchment. In a large bowl, beat the butter or margarine and sugar together with a wooden spoon until light and creamy. Beat in the eggs a little at a time, then stir in the melted chocolate.

3 Sift the flour and cocoa together and gently fold into the chocolate mixture with a metal spoon or rubber spatula.

Add the shredded coconut and mix lightly. Divide between the 2 prepared pans and smooth the tops.

4 Bake in the preheated oven for 25–30 minutes or until a skewer comes out clean when inserted into the center of the cake. Let cool in the pan for 5 minutes, then turn out, discard the lining paper, and leave on a wire rack until cool.

5 Beat together the butter or margarine and creamed coconut until fluffy. Add the confectioners' sugar and mix well. Spread half of the frosting on 1 layer and press the cakes together. Spread the remaining frosting over the top, sprinkle with the shredded coconut, and serve.

INGREDIENTS
Cuts into 8 slices

4 oz. semisweet chocolate, roughly chopped
¾ cup butter or margarine
¾ granulated sugar
3 medium eggs, beaten
1½ cups self-rising flour
1 tbsp. cocoa
¾ cup shredded coconut

FOR THE FROSTING:
½ cup butter or margarine
2 tbsp. creamed coconut
2 cups confectioners' sugar
⅓ cup shredded coconut, lightly toasted

Tasty Tip

Why not experiment with the chocolate in this recipe? For a different taste, try using orange-flavored dark chocolate or add 1–2 tablespoons of rum when melting the chocolate.

Citrus Cake

1 Preheat the oven to 170° F. Lightly grease and line the base of a round 8-inch cake pan with nonstick baking parchment.

2 In a large bowl, cream the sugar and butter or margarine together until light and fluffy. Beat the eggs together, and beat into the creamed mixture a little at a time.

3 Beat in the orange juice with 1 tablespoon of the flour. Sift the remaining flour onto a large plate several times, then with a metal spoon or rubber spatula, fold into the creamed mixture.

4 Spoon into the prepared cake pan. Stir the finely grated orange rind into the lemon curd, and dot randomly across the top of the mixture.

5 Using a fine skewer, swirl the lemon curd through the cake mixture. Bake in the preheated oven for 35 minutes until risen and golden. Allow to cool for 5 minutes in the pan, then turn out carefully onto a wire rack.

6 Sift the confectioners' sugar into a bowl, add the grated lemon rind and juice, and stir well to mix. When the cake is cool, cover the top with the icing, and serve.

INGREDIENTS
Cuts into 6 slices

¾ cup brown sugar
¾ cup butter or margarine
3 medium eggs
2 tbsp. orange juice
1½ cups self-rising flour
finely grated rind of 2 oranges
5 tbsp. lemon curd (available from specialty grocery stores)
1 scant cup confectioners' sugar
finely grated rind of 1 lemon
1 tbsp. freshly squeezed lemon juice

Food Fact

Repeated sifting, as in step 3, removes impurities from the flour while adding air to it. Using brown sugar gives a richer, sweeter taste than normal granulated sugar, and contrasts particularly well with the citrus flavor in this cake.

Victoria Sponge Cake with Mango & Mascarpone

1 Preheat the oven to 375° F. Lightly grease 2 7-inch layer-cake pans, and lightly dust with granulated sugar and flour, tapping the pans to remove any excess.

2 In a large bowl, cream the butter or margarine and sugar together with a wooden spoon until light and creamy.

3 In another bowl, mix the eggs and vanilla extract together. Sift the flour several times onto a plate.

4 Beat a little egg into the butter and sugar, then add a little flour and beat well.

5 Continue adding the flour and eggs alternately, beating between each addition until the mixture is well mixed and smooth. Divide the mixture between the 2 prepared cake pans, level the surface, then using the back of a large spoon, make a slight dip in the center of each cake.

6 Bake in the preheated oven for 25–30 minutes until the center of the cake springs back when gently pressed with a clean finger. Turn out onto a wire rack and leave the cakes until cool.

7 Beat the confectioners' sugar and mascarpone cheese together, then chop the mango into small cubes.

8 Use half the mascarpone and mango to sandwich the cakes together. Spread the rest of the mascarpone on top, decorate with the remaining mango, and serve. Otherwise, lightly cover and store in the refrigerator. Use within 3–4 days.

INGREDIENTS
Cuts into 8 slices

¾ cup granulated sugar, plus extra for dusting

1½ cups self-rising flour, plus extra for dusting

¾ cup butter or margarine

3 large eggs

1 tsp. vanilla extract

2 ½ tbsp. confectioners' sugar

9 oz. mascarpone cheese

1 large ripe mango, peeled

Tasty Tip

Mango has been used in this recipe, but mashed strawberries could be used instead. Set aside a few whole strawberries, slice, and use to decorate the cake.

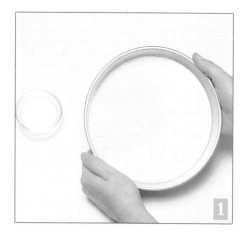

Toffee Apple Cake

1 Preheat the oven to 180° F. Lightly grease and line the bases of 2 8-inch layer-cake pans with nonstick baking parchment.

2 Thinly slice the apples and toss in the brown sugar until well coated. Arrange them over the base of the prepared pans, and set aside.

3 Cream together the butter or margarine and granulated sugar until light and fluffy.

4 Beat the eggs together in a small bowl, and gradually beat them into the creamed mixture, beating well between each addition.

5 Sift the flour into the mixture and, using a metal spoon or rubber spatula, fold in.

6 Divide the mixture between the 2 cake pans and level the surface.

7 Bake in the preheated oven for 25–30 minutes until golden and well risen. Leave in the pans to cool.

8 Lightly whip the cream with 1 tablespoon of the confectioners' sugar and the vanilla extract.

9 Sandwich the cakes together with the cream. Mix the rest of the sugar and ground cinnamon together, sprinkle over the top of the cake, and serve.

INGREDIENTS
Cuts into 8 slices

2 small apples, peeled
4 tbsp. dark brown sugar
¾ cup butter or margarine
¾ cup granulated sugar
3 medium eggs
1½ cups self-rising flour
⅔ cup heavy cream
2 tbsp. confectioners' sugar
½ tsp. vanilla extract
½ tsp. ground cinnamon

Tasty Tip

The dark brown sugar used in this recipe could be replaced with a golden brown sugar to give a deliciously rich toffee flavor to the apples. When baked, the sugar will melt slightly into a caramel consistency.

Cappuccino Cakes

1 Preheat the oven to 375° F. Place 6 large paper baking cups in a muffin pan, or place them on a cookie sheet.

2 Cream the butter or margarine and sugar together until light and fluffy. Break the eggs into a small bowl, and beat lightly with a fork.

3 Using a wooden spoon, beat the eggs into the butter and sugar mixture, a little at a time, until they are all incorporated.

4 If the mixture looks curdled, beat in a spoonful of the flour to return the mixture to a smooth consistency. Finally, beat in the black coffee.

5 Sift the flour into the mixture, then with a metal spoon or rubber spatula, gently fold in the flour.

6 Place spoonfuls of the mixture in the baking cups.

7 Bake in the preheated oven for 20–25 minutes or until risen and springy to the touch. Cool on a wire rack.

8 In a small bowl, beat together the mascarpone cheese, confectioners' sugar, and vanilla extract.

9 When the cakes are cool, spoon the vanilla mascarpone on top. Dust with cocoa and serve. Eat within 24 hours and store in the refrigerator.

INGREDIENTS
Makes 6

½ cup butter or margarine
½ cup granulated sugar
2 medium eggs
1 tbsp. strong black coffee
1¼ cups self-rising flour
¼ lb. mascarpone cheese
1 tbsp. confectioners' sugar, sifted
1 tsp. vanilla extract
sifted cocoa, to dust

Tasty Tip

The combination of coffee with the vanilla-flavored mascarpone is heavenly! Make sure, however, that you use a good-quality coffee in this recipe. Colombian coffee is generally good, and at its best, possesses a smooth, rounded flavor.

4

6

9

Honey Cake

1 Preheat the oven to 350°F. Lightly grease and line the base of a 7-inch round cake pan with lightly greased baking parchment.

2 In a saucepan, gently heat the butter, sugar, and honey until the butter has just melted.

3 Sift the flour, baking soda, and pumpkin pie spice together into a bowl.

4 Beat the egg and the milk until mixed thoroughly.

5 Make a well in the center of the sifted flour and pour in the melted butter and honey.

6 Using a wooden spoon, beat well, gradually drawing in the flour from the sides of the bowl.

7 When all the flour has been beaten in, add the egg mixture, and mix thoroughly. Pour into the prepared pan and sprinkle with the slivered almonds.

8 Bake in the preheated oven for 30–35 minutes or until well risen and golden brown, and a skewer inserted into the center of the cake comes out clean.

9 Remove from the oven, cool for a few minutes in the pan, turn out, and allow to cool on a wire rack. Drizzle with the remaining tablespoon of honey, and serve.

INGREDIENTS
Makes into 6 slices

4 tbsp. butter
2 tbsp. granulated sugar
⅓ cup honey
1½ cups all-purpose flour
½ tsp. baking soda
½ tsp. pumpkin pie spice
1 medium egg
2 tbsp. milk
¼ cup slivered almonds
1 tbsp. honey, to drizzle

Tasty Tip

Serve a slice of this cake with a large spoonful of plain yogurt on the side. The tart taste of the yogurt complements the sweetness of the honey and spice perfectly—ideal for an afternoon treat!

Fruit Cake

1 Preheat the oven to 300° F. Lightly grease and line a 9-inch round cake pan with a double thickness of waxed paper.

2 In a large bowl, cream together the butter or margarine, sugar, and orange rind until light and fluffy, then beat in the molasses.

3 Beat in the eggs, a little at a time, beating well between each addition.

4 Set aside 1 tablespoon of the flour. Sift the remaining flour, the spices, and baking soda into the mixture.

5 Mix all the fruits and the remaining flour together, then stir into the cake mixture.

6 Turn into the prepared pan and smooth the top, making a small hollow in the center of the cake mixture.

7 Bake in the preheated oven for 1 hour, then reduce the heat to 275° F.

8 Bake for an additional 1½ hours or until cooked and a skewer inserted into the center comes out clean. Let cool in the pan, then turn the cake out, and serve. Otherwise, when cool, store in an airtight container.

INGREDIENTS
Cuts into 10 slices

1 cup. butter or margarine
1 cup (scant) brown sugar
finely grated rind of 1 orange
1 tbsp. molasses
3 large eggs, beaten
2 ½ cups all-purpose flour
¼ tsp. ground cinnamon
½ tsp. pumpkin pie spice
pinch of freshly grated nutmeg
¼ tsp. baking soda
½ cup mixed candied peel
¼ cup candied cherries
⅔ cup raisins
⅔ cup golden raisins
⅔ cup dried apricots, chopped

Tasty Tip

For a fruit cake with a kick, remove the cake from the oven when cooked, and let it cool. When the cake has cooled, turn out and make holes in the base of the cake with a skewer. Dribble over 4–5 tablespoons of your favorite liquor, such as whiskey, brandy, or Drambuie.

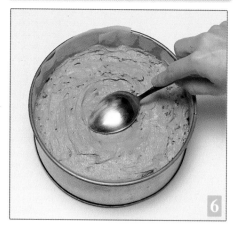

Gingerbread

1 Preheat the oven to 300° F. Lightly grease and line the base of an 8-inch round cake pan with waxed paper or baking parchment.

2 In a saucepan, gently heat the butter or margarine, molasses, and sugar, stirring occasionally until the butter melts. Let cool slightly.

3 Sift the flour and ground ginger into a large bowl.

4 Make a well in the center, then pour in the molasses mixture. Set aside 1 tablespoon of the milk, then pour the rest into the molasses mixture. Stir together lightly until mixed.

5 Beat the eggs together, then stir into the mixture.

6 Dissolve the baking soda in the remaining 1 tablespoon of warmed milk, and add to the mixture.

7 Beat the mixture until well mixed and free of lumps.

8 Pour into the prepared pan, and bake in the preheated oven for 1 hour or until well risen and a skewer inserted into the center comes out clean.

9 Cool in the pan, then remove. Slice the stem ginger into thin slivers, and sprinkle over the cake. Drizzle with the syrup and serve.

INGREDIENTS
Cuts into 8 slices

¾ cup butter or margarine
⅔ cup molasses
¼ cup brown sugar
3 cups all-purpose flour
2 tsp. ground ginger
⅔ cup milk, warmed
2 medium eggs
1 tsp. baking soda
1 piece of stem ginger in syrup
1 tbsp. stem ginger syrup

Food Fact

There are many different types of gingerbread, ranging in color from a deep, rich, dark brown to a light gold. This is due to the type of molasses and the amount of baking soda used. One type of gingerbread from Yorkshire in England is Parkin, which uses both light corn syrup and molasses.

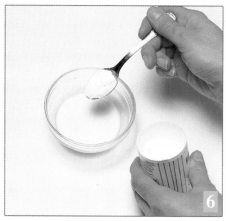

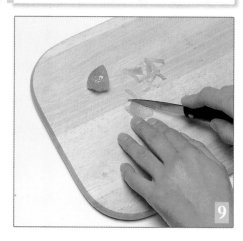

Carrot Cake

1 Preheat the oven to 300° F. Lightly grease and line the base of a 6-inch square cake pan with waxed paper or baking parchment.

2 Sift the flour, spices, baking powder, and baking soda together into a large bowl.

3 Stir in the brown sugar and mix together.

4 Lightly beat the oil and eggs together, then gradually stir into the flour and sugar mixture. Stir well.

5 Add the carrots and walnuts. Mix thoroughly, then pour into the prepared cake pan. Bake in the preheated oven for 1¼

hours or until light and springy to the touch and a skewer inserted into the center of the cake comes out clean.

6 Remove from the oven and allow to cool for 5 minutes before turning out onto a wire rack. Set aside until cool.

7 To make the frosting, beat together the cream cheese, orange rind, orange juice, and vanilla extract. Sift the confectioners' sugar and stir into the cream cheese mixture.

8 When cool, discard the lining paper, spread the cream cheese frosting over the top, and serve cut into squares.

INGREDIENTS
Cuts into 8 slices

1¾ cups all-purpose flour
½ tsp. ground cinnamon
½ tsp. freshly grated nutmeg
1 tsp. baking powder
1 tsp. baking soda
⅔ cup brown sugar
1 scant cup vegetable oil
3 medium eggs
½ lb. carrots, peeled and roughly
  grated
½ cup chopped walnuts

FOR THE FROSTING
¾ cup cream cheese
finely grated rind of 1 orange
1 tbsp. orange juice
1 tsp. vanilla extract
1 cup confectioners' sugar

Tasty Tip

For a fruitier cake, add 1 grated apple and ⅓ cup of golden raisins in step 5. To plump up the raisins, soak for an hour or overnight in a cup of cold tea.

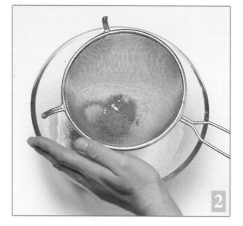

Jammy Buns

1 Preheat the oven to 375° F. Lightly grease a large cookie sheet.

2 Sift the flours and baking powder together into a large bowl, then pour in the grains remaining in the sieve.

3 Cut the butter or margarine into small pieces. (It is easier to do this when the butter is in the flour, since it helps keep the butter from sticking to the knife.)

4 Rub the butter into the flour until it resembles coarse bread crumbs. Stir in the sugar and cranberries.

5 Using a knife, stir in the beaten egg and milk. Mix to form a firm dough. Divide the mixture into 12, and roll into balls.

6 Place the dough balls on the baking tray, leaving enough space for expansion. Press your thumb into the center of each ball, making a small hollow.

7 Spoon a little of the jelly into each hollow. Pinch lightly to seal the tops.

8 Bake in the preheated oven for 20–25 minutes or until golden brown. Cool on a wire rack and serve.

INGREDIENTS
Makes 12

1½ cups all-purpose flour
1¼ cups whole-wheat flour
2 tsp. baking powder
½ cup plus 2 tbsp. butter or margarine
½ cup brown sugar
⅓ cup dried cranberries
1 large egg, beaten
1 tbsp. milk
4–5 tbsp. raspberry jelly

Tasty Tip

In this recipe, any type of jelly can be used. However, look for one with a high fruit content. Alternatively, replace the jelly with a fruit compote. Simply boil some fruit with a little sugar and water, then allow it to cool before placing inside the buns.

Whisked Sponge Cake

1 Preheat the oven to 400° F. Mix 1 teaspoon of the flour and 1 teaspoon of the sugar together. Lightly grease two 7-inch layer-cake pans and dust lightly with the sugar and flour.

2 Place the eggs in a large heatproof bowl. Add the sugar, then place over a saucepan of gently simmering water, making sure that the base of the bowl does not touch the hot water. Use an electric mixer to beat the sugar and eggs until they become light and fluffy. (The whisks should leave a trail in the mixture when lifted out.)

3 Remove the bowl from the saucepan of water, add the vanilla extract, and continue beating for 2–3 minutes. Sift the flour gently into the egg mixture and, using a metal spoon or rubber spatula, carefully fold in, taking care not to overmix and remove all the air that has been beaten in.

4 Divide the mixture between the two prepared cake pans. Tap lightly on the work surface to remove any air bubbles. Bake in the preheated oven for 20–25 minutes or until golden. Test that the cake is ready by gently pressing the center with a clean finger—it should spring back.

5 Let cool for 5 minutes, then turn out onto a wire rack. Blend the jelly and the crushed raspberries together. When the cakes are cold, spread over the jelly mixture and sandwich together. Dust the top with confectioners' sugar, and serve.

INGREDIENTS
Cuts into 6 slices

1 cup all-purpose flour, plus 1 tsp.
¾ cup granulated sugar,
    plus 1 tsp.
3 medium eggs
1 tsp. vanilla extract
4 tbsp. raspberry jelly
½ cup fresh raspberries, crushed
confectioners' sugar, to dust

Tasty Tip

For a creamier, low-fat filling, mix the crushed berries with 4 tablespoons each of low-fat, plain yogurt and low-fat crème fraîche or sour cream.

Marble Cake

1 Preheat the oven to 375° F. Lightly grease and line the base of an 8-inch round cake pan with waxed paper or baking parchment.

2 In a large bowl, cream the butter or margarine and sugar together until light and fluffy.

3 Beat the eggs together. Beat into the creamed mixture, a little at a time, beating well between each addition. When all the egg has been added, fold in the flour with a metal spoon or rubber spatula.

4 Divide the mixture equally between 2 bowls. Beat the grated orange rind into one of the bowls with a little of the orange juice. Mix the cocoa with the remaining orange juice until smooth, then add to the other bowl and beat well.

5 Spoon the mixture into the prepared pan, in alternate spoonfuls. When all the cake mixture is in the pan, take a skewer and swirl in the 2 mixtures.

6 Tap the base of the pan on the work surface to level the mixture. Bake in the preheated oven for 50 minutes or until cooked and a skewer inserted into the center of the cake comes out clean.

7 Remove from the oven and leave in the pan for a few minutes before cooling on a wire rack. Discard the lining paper.

8 For the topping, place the orange zest and juice with the granulated sugar in a small saucepan, and heat gently until the sugar has dissolved.

9 Bring to a boil and simmer gently for 3–4 minutes until the juice is syrupy. Pour over the cooled cake, and serve when cool. Otherwise, store the marble cake in an airtight container.

INGREDIENTS
Cuts into 8 slices

1 cup butter or margarine
1 cup granulated sugar
4 medium eggs
2 cups self-rising flour, sifted
finely grated rind and juice of
   1 orange
3 tbsp. cocoa, sifted

FOR THE TOPPING:
zest and juice of 1 orange
1 tbsp. granulated sugar

Helpful Hint

This cake has a wonderful combination of rich chocolate and orangey sponge. It is important not to swirl too much in step 2, since the desired effect is to have a multicolored cake.

Chocolate Chip Cookies

1 Preheat the oven to 375° F. Lightly grease a large cookie sheet.

2 In a large bowl, sift together the flour, salt, baking powder, and baking soda.

3 Cut the butter or margarine into small pieces and add to the flour mixture.

4 Using 2 knives or your fingertips, cut or rub in the butter or margarine until the mixture resembles coarse bread crumbs.

5 Add the brown sugar, corn syrup, and chocolate chips. Mix together until a smooth dough forms.

6 Shape the mixture into small balls, and arrange on the cookie sheet, leaving enough space to allow them to expand. (These cookies do not increase much in size, but allow a little space for expansion.)

7 Flatten the mixture slightly with your fingertips or the heel of your hand.

8 Bake in the preheated oven for 12–15 minutes or until golden and cooked through.

9 Allow to cool slightly, then transfer the cookies onto a rack to cool. Serve when cool, or otherwise store in an airtight container.

INGREDIENTS
Makes 36 cookies

1½ cups all-purpose flour
pinch of salt
1 tsp. baking powder
¼ tsp. baking soda
6 tbsp. butter or margarine
4 tbsp. light brown sugar
3 tbsp. light corn syrup
¾ cup chocolate chips

Tasty Tip

This is a basic cookie recipe to which many ingredients, like nuts, candied cherries, butterscotch chips, banana chips, dried cranberries, or raisins, can be added instead of chocolate chips.

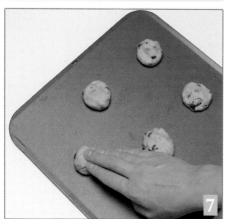

Chocolate Florentines

1 Preheat the oven to 350° F. Lightly grease a cookie sheet.

2 Melt the butter or margarine with the sugar and heavy cream in a small saucepan over a very low heat. Do not boil.

3 Remove from the heat and stir in the almonds, golden raisins, hazelnuts, and cherries.

4 Drop teaspoonfuls of the mixture onto the cookie sheet. Transfer to the preheated oven and bake for 10 minutes until golden.

5 Let cool for about 5 minutes, then carefully transfer to a wire rack.

6 Melt the semisweet, milk, and white chocolates in separate bowls, either in the microwave, following the manufacturers' instructions, or in a small bowl placed over a saucepan of gently simmering water.

7 Spread one third of the cookies with the semisweet chocolate, one third with the milk chocolate, and one third with the white chocolate.

8 Mark out wavy lines on the chocolate when almost set with the tines of a fork. Or dip some of the cookies halfway in the chocolate, and serve.

INGREDIENTS
Makes 20

½ cup butter or margarine

½ cup light brown sugar

1 tbsp. heavy cream

½ cup blanched almonds, roughly chopped

½ cup hazelnuts, roughly chopped

½ cup golden raisins

¼ cup candied cherries, roughly chopped

2 squares semisweet chocolate, roughly chopped or broken

2 oz. milk chocolate, roughly chopped or broken

2 oz. white chocolate, roughly chopped or broken

Helpful Hint

When melting chocolate for coating, as in this recipe, it is important not to overheat it or it will develop a white bloom when it resets. If melting the chocolate over simmering water, make sure the bottom of the bowl is not touching the water. If using the microwave, melt in short bursts, stirring in between to make sure that melting is even.

Tasty Tip

Rich and fruity, these Florentines rely on their raw ingredients, so try to use a good quality chocolate and natural candied cherries, which have a fruitier taste and a more natural color.

Ginger Snaps

1 Preheat the oven to 375° F. Lightly grease a cookie sheet.

2 Cream together the butter or margarine and the sugar until light and fluffy.

3 Warm the molasses in the microwave for 30–40 seconds, then add gradually to the butter mixture with the egg. Beat until well mixed.

4 In a separate bowl, sift the flour, baking soda, salt, ground ginger, ground cloves, and cinnamon. Add to the butter mixture and mix together to form a firm dough

5 Chill in the refrigerator for 1 hour. Shape the dough into small balls, and roll in the granulated sugar. Place well apart on the greased cookie sheet.

6 Sprinkle the cookie sheet with a little water and transfer to the preheated oven.

7 Bake for 12 minutes until golden and crisp. Transfer to a wire rack to cool, and serve.

INGREDIENTS
Makes 40

1 cup plus 6 tbsp. butter or margarine, softened

1 cup light brown sugar

3 tbsp. molasses

1 medium egg

3½ cups all-purpose flour

2 tsp. baking soda

½ tsp. salt

1 tsp. ground ginger

1 tsp. ground cloves

1 tsp. ground cinnamon

4 tbsp. granulated sugar

Tasty Tip

Ginger snaps are great cookies to use in other recipes. Try crushing them, mixing with melted butter, and using as the base for a cheesecake.

Tasty Tip

Ginger snaps are also delicious roughly broken up and added to homemade ice cream—particularly ginger or chocolate ice cream.

Oatmeal-Raisin Cookies

1 Preheat the oven to 400° F. Lightly grease a cookie sheet.

2 Mix together the flour, oats, ground ginger, baking powder, baking soda, sugar, and the raisins in a large bowl.

3 In another bowl, mix the egg, oil, and milk together. Make a well in the center of the dry ingredients, and pour in the egg mixture. Mix until you have a soft, but not sticky, dough.

4 Place spoonfuls of the dough well apart on the greased cookie sheet, and flatten the tops down slightly with the tines of a fork.

5 Transfer the cookies to the preheated oven, and bake for 10–12 minutes until golden.

6 Remove from the oven, let cool on the tray for 2–3 minutes, then transfer the cookies to a rack to cool. Serve when cold, or store in an airtight container.

INGREDIENTS
Makes 24

1½ cups all-purpose flour
2 cups rolled oats
1 tsp. ground ginger
½ tsp. baking powder
½ tsp. baking soda
½ cup light brown sugar
⅓ cup raisins
1 medium egg, lightly beaten
⅔ cup vegetable or sunflower oil
4 tbsp. milk

Food Fact

This dough can be made, wrapped in plastic wrap, and stored in the refrigerator for up to 1 week before baking. When ready to bake, simply cut off the dough and bake as above.

Food Fact

If desired, add ½ cup of roughly chopped mixed nuts and replace half of the raisins with dried cranberries or cherries.

Almond Macaroons

1 Preheat the oven to 300° F. Line a cookie sheet with rice paper.

2 Mix the granulated sugar, ground almonds, ground rice, and almond extract together, and set aside.

3 Beat the egg white until stiff, then gently fold in the granulated sugar mixture with a metal spoon or rubber spatula.

4 Mix to form a stiff, but not sticky, paste. If the mixture is very sticky, add a little extra ground almonds.

5 Place small spoonfuls of the mixture, about the size of an apricot, well apart on the rice paper.

6 Place half of a blanched almond in the center of each. Place in the preheated oven, and bake for 25 minutes or until just pale golden.

7 Remove the cookies from the oven and let cool for a few minutes on the cookie sheet. Cut or tear the rice paper around the macaroons to release them. Serve when cool, or store them in an airtight container.

INGREDIENTS
Makes 12

rice paper
½ cup granulated sugar
½ cup ground almonds
1 tsp. ground rice
2–3 drops almond extract
1 medium egg white
8 blanched almonds, halved

Tasty Tip

Rice paper is an edible paper made from the pith of the Chinese tree. These macaroons are deliciously chewy and are fantastic when broken up and sprinkled in desserts such as trifles. Serve with cream and tart, fresh fruits, such as raspberries.

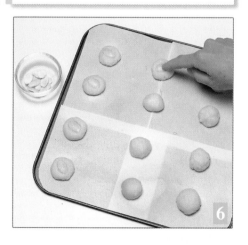

Pumpkin Cookies with Brown Butter Glaze

1 Preheat the oven to 375° F. Lightly grease a cookie sheet, and set aside.

2 Using an electric mixer, beat the butter until light and fluffy. Add the flour, sugar, pumpkin, beaten egg, and beat with the mixer until mixed well.

3 Stir in the ground cinnamon and 1 teaspoon of the vanilla extract, then sift in the baking powder, baking soda, and grated nutmeg. Beat the mixture until combined well, scraping down the sides of the bowl.

4 Add the whole-wheat flour, chopped nuts, and raisins to the mixture, and fold in with a metal spoon or rubber spatula until mixed thoroughly.

5 Place teaspoonfuls about 2 inches apart on the cookie sheet. Bake in the preheated oven for 10–12 minutes or until the cookie edges are firm.

6 Remove the cookies from the oven and let cool on a wire rack. Meanwhile, melt the butter in a small saucepan over a medium heat until pale and just turning golden brown.

7 Remove from the heat. Add the sugar, the remaining vanilla extract, and milk, stirring. Drizzle over the cooled cookies and serve.

INGREDIENTS
Makes 48

½ cup butter, softened
1¼ cup all-purpose flour
¾ cup light brown sugar, lightly packed
1⅓ cups canned pumpkin or cooked pumpkin
1 medium egg, beaten
2 tsp. ground cinnamon
2½ tsp. vanilla extract
½ tsp. baking powder
½ tsp. baking soda
½ tsp. freshly grated nutmeg
½ cup whole-wheat flour
¾ cup pecans, roughly chopped
½ cup raisins
4 tbsp. unsalted butter
2 cups confectioners' sugar
2 tbsp. milk

Helpful Hint

To cook pumpkin, take a slice off the top of the pumpkin. Scrape out the seeds and discard. Cut the pumpkin vertically into quarters and remove the dark orange skin with a potato peeler. Cut the flesh into chunks, and steam or microwave until tender. Purée to use in the above recipe.

Spiced Palmiers with Apple Sauce

1 Preheat the oven to 400° F. Roll out the pastry on a lightly floured surface to form a 10 x 12 inch rectangle. Trim the edges with a small, sharp knife.

2 Sift together the granulated sugar, confectioners' sugar, cinnamon, ginger, and nutmeg into a bowl. Dust both sides of a pastry board with about a quarter of the sugar mixture.

3 With a long edge facing your body, fold either side halfway toward the center. Dust with a third of the remaining sugar mixture.

4 Fold each side again so that they almost meet in the center, and dust again with about half the remaining sugar mixture. Fold the 2 sides together down the center of the pastry to give 6 layers altogether. Wrap the pastry in plastic wrap, and refrigerate for 1–2 hours until firm. Set aside the remaining spiced sugar.

5 Remove the pastry from the refrigerator, unwrap, and roll in the remaining sugar to give a good coating all over. Using a sharp knife, cut the roll into about 20 thin slices. Place cut-side down onto a cookie sheet, and place in the preheated oven.

6 Cook for 10 minutes, turn the cookies, and cook for an additional 5–10 minutes or until golden and crisp. Remove from the oven, and transfer to a wire rack. Allow to cool completely.

7 Meanwhile, combine the rest of the ingredients in a saucepan. Cover and cook gently for 15 minutes until the apple is completely soft. Stir well and allow to cool. Serve the palmiers with a spoonful of the apple sauce and a little of the whipped cream.

INGREDIENTS
Makes 20

generous ½ lb. prepared puff
  pastry, thawed if frozen
3 tbsp. granulated sugar
2 tbsp. confectioners' sugar
1 tsp. ground cinnamon
¼ tsp. ground ginger
¼ tsp. freshly grated nutmeg
1 lb. apples, roughly chopped
4 tbsp. sugar
¼ cup raisins
¼ cup dried cherries
zest of 1 orange
heavy cream, lightly whipped,
  to serve

Food Fact
Palmiers are so called because they resemble palm leaves—*palmier* being the French word for a palm tree. Palmiers are often served sandwiched together with whipped cream and jelly.

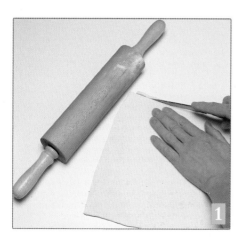

Oatmeal-Coconut Cookies

1 Preheat the oven to 350° F. Lightly grease a cookie sheet.

2 Cream together the butter or margarine and sugars until light and fluffy.

3 Gradually stir in the egg and vanilla extract, and beat until well blended.

4 Sift together the flour, baking powder, and baking soda in another bowl.

5 Add to the butter and sugar mixture, and beat together until smooth. Fold in the rolled oats and coconut with a metal spoon or rubber spatula.

6 Roll heaping teaspoonfuls of the mixture into balls and place on the cookie sheet about 2 inches apart, and flatten each ball slightly with the heel of the hand.

7 Transfer to the preheated oven and bake for 12–15 minutes until just golden.

8 Remove from the oven and transfer the cookies to a wire rack to cool completely, and serve.

INGREDIENTS
Makes 40

1 cup butter or margarine
½ cup light brown sugar
½ cup granulated sugar
1 large egg, lightly beaten
1 tsp. vanilla extract
2 cups all-purpose flour
1 tsp. baking powder
½ tsp. baking soda
1¼ cups rolled oats
1 cup shredded coconut

Helpful Hint

The leavening agent in this recipe, baking soda, lightens the texture of these cookies, resulting in a crisp cookie that will melt in your mouth. These cookies will last for 3–4 days if stored in an airtight container.

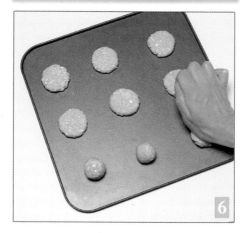

Miracle Bars

1 Preheat the oven to 350° F. Butter a 9-inch square pan and line with a layer of nonstick baking parchment.

2 Pour the butter into the prepared pan, and sprinkle the graham cracker crumbs over in an even layer.

3 Add the chocolate chips, coconut, and nuts in even layers and drizzle over the condensed milk.

4 Transfer the pan to the preheated oven, and bake for 30 minutes until golden brown. Allow to cool in the pan, then cut into 12 squares, and serve.

INGREDIENTS
Makes 12

7 tbsp. butter, melted, plus 1–2 tsp. extra for greasing

1½ cups graham cracker crumbs

¾ cup chocolate chips

1 cup shredded coconut

1 cup chopped mixed nuts

16-oz. can sweetened condensed milk

Food Fact

Condensed milk is pasteurized, homogenized milk that has been reduced to about two-thirds of its original volume by boiling under strictly controlled conditions. It is no longer advised to boil the can of condensed milk to convert the milk to a golden toffee filling due to the risk of an explosion. Instead, either place the milk in a heavy-based saucepan and boil gently, or place in a glass bowl, cover with plastic wrap, pierce, and cook on medium for 1–2 minutes at a time in a microwave. Keep checking to make sure the milk does not burn.

Apple & Cinnamon Crumble Bars

1 Preheat the oven to 375° F. Place the apples, raisins, sugar, cinnamon, and lemon zest into a saucepan over a low heat.

2 Cover and cook for about 15 minutes, stirring occasionally, until the apple is cooked through. Remove the cover and stir well, using a wooden spoon, to break up the apple completely.

3 Cook for an additional 15–30 minutes over a very low heat until reduced, thickened, and slightly darkened. Allow to cool. Lightly grease and line an 8-inch square cake pan with waxed paper or baking parchment.

4 Mix together the flour, sugar, baking soda, rolled oats, and butter until combined well and crumbly.

5 Spread half of the flour mixture into the bottom of the prepared pan and press down. Pour over the apple mixture.

6 Sprinkle over the remaining flour mixture, and press down lightly. Bake in the preheated oven for 30–35 minutes until golden brown.

7 Remove from the oven and allow to cool before cutting into slices. Serve the bars warm or cold with crème fraîche or whipped cream.

INGREDIENTS
Makes 16

1 lb. apples, roughly chopped
⅓ cup raisins
4 tbsp. granulated sugar
1 tsp. ground cinnamon
zest of 1 lemon
1¾ cups all-purpose flour
1¼ cups light brown sugar
½ tsp. baking soda
2 cups rolled oats
½ cup plus 2 tbsp. butter, melted
crème fraîche or whipped cream,
  to serve

Tasty Tip

The apple filling in this recipe is very similar to apple butter. To make apple butter, cook the filling in step 2 for an additional 30 minutes over a very low heat, stirring often. When reduced to one-third of its original volume (it should be quite dark), then it is ready. It is also delicious spread on toast.

Lemon Bars

1 Preheat the oven to 325° F. Lightly grease and line an 8-inch square cake pan with waxed paper or baking parchment.

2 Rub together the flour and butter until the mixture resembles bread crumbs. Stir in 4 tablespoons of the granulated sugar, and mix.

3 Press the mixture down firmly into the prepared pan. Bake in the preheated oven for 20 minutes until pale golden.

4 Meanwhile, in a food processor, mix together the remaining sugar, flour, baking powder, salt, eggs, lemon juice, and lemon rind until smooth. Pour over the prepared base.

5 Transfer to the preheated oven and bake for an additional 20–25 minutes until nearly set. Remove from the oven, and cool in the pan on a wire rack.

6 Dust with confectioners' sugar, and cut into squares. Serve cool, or store in an airtight container.

INGREDIENTS
Makes 24

1½ cups all-purpose flour
½ cup butter
1 cup plus 2 tbsp. granulated sugar
2 tbsp. flour
½ tsp. baking powder
¼ tsp. salt
2 medium eggs, lightly beaten
juice and finely grated rind of 1 lemon
sifted confectioners' sugar, to decorate

Food Fact

Baking powder is a chemically prepared leavening agent consisting of cream of tartar and baking soda, which is then mixed with a dried starch or flour. It is very important to measure accurately, otherwise the mixture could either not rise, or rise too quickly and then collapse, giving a sour taste to the dish.

Lemon-Iced Ginger Squares

1 Preheat the oven to 400° F. Lightly grease an 8-inch square cake pan and sprinkle with a little flour.

2 Mix together the granulated sugar, butter, and molasses. Stir in the egg whites.

3 Mix together the flour, baking soda, cloves, cinnamon, ginger, and salt.

4 Stir the flour mixture and buttermilk alternately into the butter mixture until well blended.

5 Spoon into the prepared pan and bake in the preheated oven for 35 minutes or until a skewer inserted into the center of the cake comes out clean.

6 Remove from the oven and allow to cool for 5 minutes in the pan before turning out onto a wire rack over a large plate. Using a toothpick, make holes on the top of the cake.

7 Meanwhile, mix together the confectioners' sugar with enough lemon juice to make a smooth, pourable frosting.

8 Carefully pour the frosting over the hot cake, then leave until cool. Cut the ginger cake into squares, and serve.

INGREDIENTS
Makes 12

1 cup granulated sugar
4 tbsp. butter, melted
2 tbsp. molasses
2 medium egg whites, lightly beaten
2 cups all-purpose flour
1 tsp. baking soda
½ tsp. ground cloves
1 tsp. ground cinnamon
¼ tsp. ground ginger
pinch of salt
1 cup buttermilk
1 cup plus 4 tbsp. confectioners' sugar
lemon juice

Food Fact

Buttermilk is the liquid that remains after churning cream into butter. It is considered a healthy alternative to sour cream, since it does not contain the fat of the cream. It contains lactic acid, and when mixed with baking soda, it acts as a rising agent.

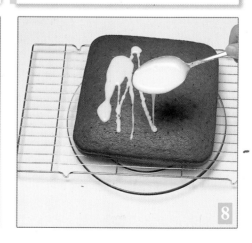

Pecan-Caramel Millionaire's Shortbread

1 Preheat the oven to 350° F. Lightly grease and line a 7 x 11 inch pan with waxed paper or baking parchment.

2 Cream together the butter, peanut butter, and sugar until light. Sift in the cornstarch and flour together, and mix in to make a smooth dough.

3 Press the mixture into the prepared pan, and prick all over with a fork. Bake in the preheated oven for 20 minutes until just golden. Remove from the oven.

4 Meanwhile, for the topping, combine the sugar, butter, light corn syrup, glucose, water, and milk in a heavy-based saucepan.

5 Stir constantly over a low heat without boiling until the sugar has dissolved. Increase the heat, boil, stirring constantly, for about 10 minutes until the mixture turns a caramel color.

6 Remove the saucepan from the heat and add the pecans. Pour over the shortbread base immediately. Allow to cool, then refrigerate for at least 1 hour.

7 Break the chocolate into small pieces and put into a heatproof bowl, along with the butter.

8 Place over a saucepan of barely simmering water, making sure that the bowl does not come into contact with the water. Leave until melted, then stir together well.

9 Remove the shortbread from the refrigerator and pour the chocolate evenly over the top, spreading thinly to cover. Leave to set, cut into squares, and serve.

INGREDIENTS
Makes 20

½ cup butter, softened
2 tbsp. smooth peanut butter
6 tbsp. granulated sugar
½ cup cornstarch
1½ cups all-purpose flour

FOR THE TOPPING:

1 cup (scant) granulated sugar
½ cup butter
2 tbsp. light corn syrup
3 tbsp. liquid glucose
6 tbsp. water
16-oz. can sweetened condensed milk
1½ cups pecans, roughly chopped
3 squares semisweet chocolate
1 tbsp. butter

Tasty Tip

Any type of nut can be used in this recipe. Why not try replacing the pecans with a variety of chopped walnuts, almonds, and brazil nuts?

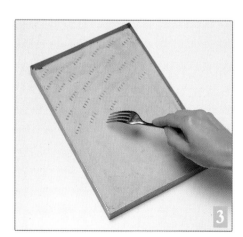

Fruit & Nut Pan Cake

1 Preheat the oven to 350°F. Lightly grease a 9-inch square cake pan.

2 Melt the butter or margarine with the sugar and syrup in a small saucepan over a low heat. Remove from the heat.

3 Stir the raisins, walnuts, and oats into the syrup mixture, and mix together.

4 Spoon the oat mixture evenly into the prepared pan and press down firmly.

Transfer to the preheated oven and bake for 20–25 minutes.

5 Remove from the oven and let cool in the pan. Cut into bars while still warm.

6 Sift the confectioners' sugar into a small bowl, then gradually beat in the lemon juice, a little at a time, to form a thin frosting.

7 Place into a piping bag fitted with a writing tip, then pipe thin lines over the flapjacks. Let cool, then serve.

INGREDIENTS
Makes 12

6 tbsp. butter or margarine
½ cup golden brown sugar
3 tbsp. corn syrup
½ cup raisins
½ cup walnuts, roughly chopped
1 scant cup rolled oats
5 tbsp. confectioners' sugar
1–1½ tbsp lemon juice

Tasty Tip

This cake is packed with energy, but why not increase the nutritional value by adding a few tablespoons of seeds, such as sesame, sunflower, and pumpkin seeds, then add some chopped-up dried fruits, such as apricot, pineapple, or mango? You can also add chocolate chips, chopped candied fruits, as well as currants and golden raisins.

Food Fact

The rolled oats used in this cake can also be used for oatmeal, as can steel-cut oats, which are an integral part of haggis, oatcakes, and the whiskey drink Athol Brose—all great Scottish dishes.

Fresh Strawberry Sponge Cake

1 Preheat the oven to 375° F. Lightly grease and line the bases of 2 8-inch round cake pans with waxed paper or baking parchment.

2 Using an electric mixer, beat the butter, sugar, and vanilla extract until pale and fluffy. Gradually beat in the eggs, a little at a time, beating well between each addition.

3 Sift half the flour over the mixture, and using a metal spoon, gently fold into the mixture. Sift over the remaining flour and fold in until just blended.

4 Divide the mixture between the pans, spreading evenly. Gently smooth the surfaces with the back of a spoon. Bake in the center of the preheated oven for 20–25 minutes or until well risen and golden.

5 Remove and let cool before turning out onto a wire rack. Whip the cream with 1 tablespoon of the confectioners' sugar until it forms soft peaks. Fold in the chopped strawberries

6 Spread 1 cake layer evenly with the mixture and top with the second cake layer, rounded-side up.

7 Dust the cake with confectioners' sugar and decorate with the remaining berries. Slide onto a serving plate, and serve.

INGREDIENTS
8–10 servings

¾ cup unsalted butter, softened
¾ cup granulated sugar
1 tsp. vanilla extract
3 large eggs, beaten
1 ½ cups self-rising flour
½ cup heavy cream
2 tbsp. confectioners' sugar, sifted
1½ cups fresh strawberries, hulled and chopped
extra strawberries, to decorate

Helpful Hint

For sponge cakes, it is important to achieve the correct consistency of the uncooked mixture. Check after folding in the flour by tapping a spoonful of the mixture on the side of the bowl. If it drops easily, "dropping" consistency has been reached. If it is stiff, add a tablespoon of cooled boiled water.

Almond Angel Food Cake with Amaretto Cream

1 Preheat the oven to 350° F. Sift together the 1½ cups confectioners' sugar and flour. Stir to blend, then sift again.

2 Using an electric mixer, beat the egg whites, cream of tartar, vanilla extract, ½ teaspoon of almond extract, and salt on medium speed until soft peaks form. Gradually add the granulated sugar, 2 tablespoons at a time, beating well after each addition until stiff peaks form.

3 Sift about one third of the flour mixture over the egg white mixture, and, using a metal spoon or rubber spatula, gently fold into the egg white mixture.

4 Repeat, folding the flour mixture into the egg white mixture in 2 more batches. Spoon into an ungreased angel food cake pan or 10-inch tube pan.

5 Bake in the preheated oven until risen and golden on top and the surface springs back quickly when gently pressed. Immediately invert the cake pan and cool completely in the pan.

6 When cool, run a sharp knife around the edge and the center ring to loosen the cake from the edge. Using the fingertips, ease the cake from the pan and invert onto a cake plate. Thickly dust the cake with the extra confectioners' sugar.

7 Whip the cream with the remaining almond extract, Amaretto liqueur, and a little more confectioners' sugar until soft peaks form.

8 Fill a piping bag fitted with a star tip with half the cream, and pipe around the bottom of the cake. Decorate the edge with the fresh raspberries, and serve the remaining cream separately.

INGREDIENTS
Cuts into 10–12 slices

1½ cups confectioners' sugar, plus 2–3 tbsp.

1¼ cups all-purpose flour

1½ cups egg whites (about 10 large egg whites)

1½ tsp. cream of tartar

½ tsp. vanilla extract

1 tsp. almond extract

¼ tsp. salt

1 scant cup granulated sugar

¾ cup heavy cream

2 tablespoons Amaretto liqueur

fresh raspberries, to decorate

Food Fact

Angel food cake has a very light and delicate texture, and can be difficult to slice. For best results, use 2 forks to gently separate a portion of the cake.

1

4

8

Luxury Carrot Cake

1 Preheat the oven to 350° F. Lightly grease a 9-inch round baking pan. Line the base with nonstick baking parchment. Grease, then dust with flour.

2 Sift the first 6 ingredients into a large bowl, and stir in the sugars to blend. Make a well in the center.

3 Beat the eggs, oil, and vanilla extract together, and pour into the well. Using an electric mixer, gradually beat, drawing in the flour mixture from the side until a smooth batter forms. Stir in the carrots, crushed pineapple, and chopped nuts until blended.

4 Pour into the prepared pan and smooth the surface evenly. Bake in the preheated oven for 50 minutes or until firm and a skewer inserted into the center comes out clean. Remove from the oven and let cool before removing from the pan and discarding the lining paper.

5 For the frosting, beat the cream cheese, butter, and vanilla extract together until smooth, then gradually beat in the confectioners' sugar until the frosting is smooth. Add a little milk, if necessary. Spread the frosting over the top. Refrigerate for 1 hour to set the frosting, then cut into squares and serve.

INGREDIENTS
Cuts into 12 slices

2½ cups all-purpose flour

2 tsp. baking powder

1 tsp. baking soda

1 tsp. salt

2 tsp. ground cinnamon

1 tsp. ground ginger

1 scant cup dark brown sugar

½ scant cup granulated sugar

4 large eggs, beaten

1 cup plus 2 tbsp. sunflower oil

1 tbsp. vanilla extract

4 carrots, peeled and grated (about 1 lb.)

14-oz. can crushed pineapple, well drained

1 cup pecans or walnuts, toasted and chopped

FOR THE FROSTING:

¾ cup cream cheese, softened

4 tbsp. butter, softened

1 tsp. vanilla extract

2 cups confectioners' sugar, sifted

1–2 tbsp. milk

Food Fact

Carrots contain beta-carotene, which converts in the body to vitamin A. This antioxidant helps in the fight against heart disease and cancer. When buying carrots, choose bright-colored, firm, well-shaped specimens, and avoid peeling them, since the vitamin content is located just under the skin.

White Chocolate Cheesecake

1 Preheat the oven to 350° F. Lightly grease a 9-inch round springform pan. Crush the graham crackers and almonds in a food processor to form fine crumbs.

2 Pour in the butter and almond extract, and blend. Pour the crumbs into the pan, and using the back of a spoon, press onto the bottom and up the sides to within ½ inch of the top of the pan edge.

3 Bake in the preheated oven for 5 minutes to set. Remove, and transfer to a wire rack. Reduce the oven temperature to 300° F.

4 Heat the white chocolate and cream in a saucepan over a low heat, stirring constantly until melted. Remove and cool.

5 Beat the cream cheese and sugar until smooth. Add the eggs, one at a time, beating well after each addition. Slowly beat in the cooled white chocolate cream and the Amaretto, and pour into the baked crust. Place on a baking tray, and bake for 45–55 minutes until the edge of the cake is firm, but the center is slightly soft. Reduce the oven temperature if the top begins to brown. Transfer to a wire rack and increase the temperature to 400° F.

6 To make the topping, beat the sour cream, sugar, and almond or vanilla extract until smooth, and gently pour over the cheesecake, tilting the pan to distribute the topping evenly. Alternatively, spread with a metal palette knife.

7 Bake for another 5 minutes to set. Turn off the oven and leave the door halfway open for about 1 hour. Transfer to a wire rack, and run a sharp knife around the edge of the crust to separate from the pan. Cool and refrigerate until chilled. Remove from the pan, decorate with white chocolate curls, and serve.

INGREDIENTS
Cuts into 16 slices

FOR THE BASE:
1⅔ cups graham crackers
½ cup whole almonds, lightly toasted
4 tbsp. butter, melted
½ tsp. almond extract

FOR THE FILLING:
12 oz. good-quality white chocolate, chopped
⅓ cup heavy cream
1½ lbs. cream cheese, softened
4 tbsp. granulated sugar
4 large eggs
2 tbsp. Amaretto or almond-flavor liqueur

FOR THE TOPPING:
2 cups sour cream
4 tbsp. granulated sugar
½ tsp. almond or vanilla extract
white chocolate curls, to decorate

Rich Devil's Food Cake

1 Preheat the oven to 350° F. Lightly grease and line the bases of three 9-inch cake pans with waxed paper or baking parchment. Sift the flour, baking soda, and salt into a bowl.

2 Sift the cocoa into another bowl and gradually beat in a little of the milk to form a paste. Continue beating in the milk until a smooth mixture results.

3 Beat the butter, sugar, and vanilla extract until light and fluffy, then gradually beat in the eggs, beating well after each addition. Stir in the flour and cocoa mixtures alternately in 3 or 4 batches.

4 Divide the mixture evenly among the 3 pans, smoothing the surfaces evenly. Bake in the preheated oven for 25-35 minutes until cooked and firm to the touch. Remove, cool, and turn out onto a wire rack. Discard the lining paper.

5 To make the frosting, put the sugar, salt, and chocolate into a heavy-based saucepan, and stir in the milk until blended. Add the light corn syrup and butter. Bring the mixture to a boil over medium-high heat, stirring to help dissolve the sugar.

6 Boil for 1 minute, stirring constantly. Remove from the heat, stir in the vanilla extract, and cool. When cool, beat until thickened and slightly lightened in color.

7 Sandwich the three cake layers together with about a third of the frosting, placing the third cake layer with the flat-side up.

8 Transfer the cake to a serving plate, and using a metal palette knife, spread the remaining frosting over the top and sides. Swirl the top to create a decorative effect, and serve.

INGREDIENTS
Cuts into 12–16 slices

4 cups all-purpose flour
1 tbsp. baking soda
½ tsp. salt
9 tbsp. unsweetened cocoa
1¼ cups milk
½ cup plus 2 tbsp. butter, softened
¾ cups dark brown sugar
2 tsp. vanilla extract
4 large eggs

CHOCOLATE FUDGE
   FROSTING:

1¼ cups granulated sugar
½ tsp. salt
4 squares semisweet chocolate, chopped
1 cup milk
2 tbsp. light corn syrup
½ cup butter, diced
2 tsp. vanilla extract

Italian Polenta Cake with Mascarpone Cream

1 Preheat the oven to 375° F. Butter a 9-inch springform pan. Dust lightly with flour.

2 Stir the flour, polenta or cornmeal, baking powder, salt, and lemon zest together. Beat the eggs and half the sugar until light and fluffy. Slowly beat in the milk and almond extract.

3 Stir in the seedless or golden raisins, then beat in the flour mixture and 4 tablespoons of the butter.

4 Spoon into the pan and smooth the top evenly. Arrange the pear slices on top in overlapping concentric circles.

5 Melt the remaining butter and brush over the pear slices. Sprinkle with the rest of the sugar.

6 Bake in the preheated oven for about 40 minutes until puffed and golden, and the edges of the pears are lightly caramelized. Transfer to a wire rack. Set aside to cool in the pan for 15 minutes.

7 Remove the cake from the pan. Heat the apricot jelly with 1 tablespoon of water and brush over the top of the cake to glaze.

8 Beat the mascarpone cheese with the sugar, the cream, and Amaretto or rum until smooth and forming a soft, dropping consistency.

9 When cool, sprinkle the almonds over the polenta cake and dust generously with the confectioners' sugar. Serve the cake with the liqueur-flavored mascarpone cream separately or on the side.

INGREDIENTS
Cuts into 6–8 slices

1 tsp. butter and flour for the pan
1 scant cup all-purpose flour
¼ cup polenta or yellow cornmeal
1 tsp. baking powder
¼ tsp. salt
grated zest of 1 lemon
2 large eggs
½ cup plus 2 tbsp. granulated sugar
5 tbsp. milk
½ tsp. almond extract
2 tbsp. seedless raisins or golden raisins
6 tbsp. unsalted butter, softened
2 medium dessert pears, peeled, cored, and thinly sliced
2 tbsp. apricot jelly
6 oz. mascarpone cheese
1–2 tsp. sugar
¼ cup heavy cream
2 tbsp. Amaretto liqueur or rum
2–3 tbsp. toasted, slivered almonds
confectioners' sugar, to dust

Fall Apple Cake

1 Preheat the oven to 325° F. Lightly grease and line the base of an 8-inch cake pan with nonstick baking parchment or waxed paper. Sift the flour and baking powder into a small bowl.

2 Beat the margarine, sugar, and vanilla extract until light and fluffy. Gradually beat in the eggs, a little at a time, beating well after each addition. Stir in the flour.

3 Spoon about one third of the mixture into the pan, smoothing the surface. Toss the apple slices in the lemon juice and cinnamon, and spoon over the cake mixture, making a thick, even layer. Spread the remaining mixture over the apple layer to the edge of the pan, making sure the apples are covered. Smooth the top with the back of a wet spoon, and sprinkle generously with sugar.

4 Bake in the preheated oven for 1½ hours or until well risen and golden, the apples are tender, and the center of the cake springs back when pressed lightly. If the top browns too quickly, reduce the oven temperature slightly and cover the cake loosely with foil.

5 Transfer to a wire rack and cool for about 20 minutes in the pan. Run a thin knife blade between the cake and the pan to loosen the cake, and invert onto a paper-lined rack. Turn the cake right-side up, and cool. Serve with the custard sauce or cream.

INGREDIENTS
Cuts into 8–10 slices

2 cups self-rising flour

1½ tsp. baking powder

½ cup plus 2 tbsp. margarine, softened

½ cup plus 2 tbsp. granulated sugar, plus extra for sprinkling

1 tsp. vanilla extract

2 large eggs, beaten

2½ lbs. apples, peeled, cored, and sliced

1 tbsp. lemon juice

½ tsp. ground cinnamon

fresh custard sauce or cream, to serve

Food Fact

Cooking apples are extremely versatile, as they can be baked, puréed, poached, and used in cakes and pies, as well as savory foods. Apples have a good soluble fiber content, making them an extremely nutritious food.

Thanksgiving Cranberry-Chocolate Roulade

1 Preheat the oven to 400° F. Bring the cream to a boil over medium heat. Remove from the heat and add all of the chocolate, stirring until melted. Stir in the brandy, if desired, and strain into a medium bowl. Cool, then refrigerate for 6–8 hours.

2 Lightly grease and line a 10 x 15 inch jelly roll pan with nonstick baking parchment. Using an electric mixer, beat the egg yolks until thick and creamy. Slowly beat in the cocoa and half the confectioners' sugar, and set aside. Beat the egg whites and tartar into soft peaks. Gradually beat in the remaining sugar until the mixture is stiff and glossy. Gently fold the yolk mixture into the egg whites with a metal spoon or rubber spatula. Spread evenly into the pan.

3 Bake in the preheated oven for 15 minutes. Remove, then invert onto a large sheet of waxed paper dusted with cocoa. Cut off the crisp edges of the cake, then roll up. Leave on a wire rack until cool.

4 For the filling, heat the cranberry sauce with the brandy, if desired, until warm and spreadable. Unroll the cooled cake and spread with the cranberry sauce. Allow to cool and set. Carefully spoon the whipped cream over the surface and spread to within 1 inch of the edges. Roll the cake again. Transfer to a cake plate or tray.

5 Allow the chocolate ganache to soften at room temperature, then beat until soft and of a spreadable consistency. Spread over the roulade, and using a fork, mark the roulade with ridges to resemble tree bark. Dust with confectioners' sugar. Decorate with the candied orange strips and dried cranberries, and serve.

INGREDIENTS
Cuts into 12–14 slices

CHOCOLATE GANACHE FROSTING:
1¼ cups heavy cream
12 squares semisweet chocolate, chopped
2 tbsp. brandy (optional)

FOR THE ROULADE:
5 large eggs, separated
3 tbsp. cocoa, sifted, plus extra for dusting
1 cup confectioners' sugar, sifted, plus extra for dusting
¼ tsp. cream of tartar

FOR THE FILLING:
¾ cup cranberry sauce
1–2 tbsp. brandy (optional)
⅔ cup heavy cream, whipped to soft peaks

TO DECORATE:
candied orange strips
dried cranberries

Buttery Passion Fruit Madeira Cake

1 Preheat the oven to 350° F. Lightly grease and line the base of a 5 x 9 inch loaf pan with waxed paper. Sift the flour and baking powder into a bowl, and set aside.

2 Beat the butter, sugar, orange zest, and vanilla extract until light and fluffy, then gradually beat in the eggs, 1 tablespoon at a time, beating well after each addition. If the mixture appears to curdle or separate, beat in a little of the flour mixture.

3 Fold in the flour mixture with the milk until just blended. Do not overmix. Spoon lightly into the prepared pan and smooth the top evenly. Sprinkle lightly with the teaspoon of granulated sugar.

4 Bake in the preheated oven for 55 minutes or until well risen and golden brown. Remove and cool for 15–20 minutes. Turn the cake out of the pan and discard the lining paper.

5 Cut the passion fruit in half, and scoop out the pulp into a sieve set over a bowl. Press the juice through using a rubber spatula or wooden spoon. Stir in the confectioners' sugar and stir to dissolve, adding a little extra sugar if necessary.

6 Using a skewer, pierce holes all over the cake. Slowly spoon the passion fruit glaze over the cake and allow it to seep in. Gently invert the cake onto a wire rack, then turn it right-side up. Dust with confectioners' sugar and cool completely. Serve cold.

INGREDIENTS
Cuts into 8–10 slices

2 scant cups all-purpose flour

1 tsp. baking powder

¾ cup sweet butter, softened

1 cup plus 2 tbsp. granulated sugar, plus 1 tsp. for sprinkling

grated zest of 1 orange

1 tsp. vanilla extract

3 medium eggs, beaten

2 tbsp. milk

6 ripe passion fruit

5 tbsp. confectioners' sugar

confectioners' sugar, to dust

Food Fact

Regardless of its name, Madeira cake does not actually originate from the Portuguese-owned island of Madeira. It is, in fact, a traditional English cake that was often served with Madeira, a fortified wine which does derive its name from the island.

French Chocolate Pecan Torte

1 Preheat the oven to 350° F. Lightly butter and line an 8-inch round pan with nonstick baking parchment. Wrap the pan in a large sheet of foil to keep water from seeping in.

2 Melt the chocolate and butter in a saucepan over a low heat and stir until smooth. Remove from the heat and cool.

3 Using an electric mixer, beat the eggs, sugar, and vanilla extract until light and foamy. Gradually beat in the melted chocolate, ground nuts, and cinnamon, then pour into the prepared pan.

4 Set the foil-wrapped pan in a large roasting pan and pour in enough boiling water to come ¾ inch up the side of the pan. Bake in the preheated oven until the edge is set but the center is still soft when the pan is gently shaken. Remove from the oven and place on a wire rack to cool.

5 For the glaze, melt all the ingredients over a low heat until melted and smooth, then remove from the heat. Dip each pecan halfway into the glaze, and set on a sheet of nonstick baking parchment until set. Allow the remaining glaze to thicken slightly.

6 Remove the cake from the pan and invert. Pour the glaze over the cake, smoothing the top and spreading the glaze around the sides. Arrange the glazed pecans around the edge of the torte. Allow to set, then serve.

INGREDIENTS
Cuts into 16 slices

7 squares semisweet chocolate, chopped

½ cup plus 2 tbsp. butter, diced

4 large eggs

½ scant cup granulated sugar

2 tsp. vanilla extract

1 cup pecans, finely ground

2 tsp. ground cinnamon

24 pecan halves, lightly toasted, to decorate

CHOCOLATE GLAZE:

4 squares semisweet chocolate, chopped

5 tbsp. butter, diced

2 tbsp. honey

¼ tsp. ground cinnamon

Food Fact

Although this recipe is French, the torte actually originates from Germany, and tends to be a very rich, cakelike dessert. It is delicious served with a fruity mixed-berry compote.

Lemony Coconut Cake

1 Preheat the oven to 350° F. Lightly grease and flour 2 8-inch, round, nonstick cake pans.

2 Sift the flour, cornstarch, baking powder, and salt into a large bowl, and add the shortening or margarine, sugar, lemon zest, vanilla extract, eggs, and milk.

3 With an electric mixer on a low speed, beat until blended, adding a little extra milk if the mixture is very stiff. Increase the speed to medium and beat for about 2 minutes.

4 Divide the mixture between the pans and smooth the tops evenly. Bake in the preheated oven for 20–25 minutes or until the cakes feel firm and are cooked. Remove from the oven, and cool before removing from the pans.

5 Put all the ingredients for the frosting, except the coconut, into a heatproof bowl placed over a saucepan of simmering water. Do not allow the base of the bowl to touch the water.

6 Using an electric mixer, blend the frosting ingredients on a low speed. Increase the speed to high, and beat for 7 minutes until the whites are stiff and glossy. Remove the bowl from the heat and continue beating until cool. Cover with plastic wrap.

7 Using a serrated knife, split the cake layers horizontally in half and sprinkle each cut surface with the Malibu or rum. Sandwich the cakes together with the lemon curd, and press lightly.

8 Spread the top and sides generously with the frosting, swirling the top. Sprinkle the coconut over the top and gently press onto the sides to cover. Decorate the coconut cake with the lime zest, and serve.

INGREDIENTS
Cuts into 10–12 slices

2½ cups all-purpose flour
2 tbsp. cornstarch
1 tbsp. baking powder
1 tsp. salt
½ cup plus 2 tbsp. shortening or soft margarine
1¼ cups granulated sugar
grated zest of 2 lemons
1 tsp. vanilla extract
3 large eggs
⅔ cup milk
4 tbsp. Malibu or rum
16-oz. jar lemon curd (available from specialty grocery stores)
lime zest, to decorate

FOR THE FROSTING:

1¼ cups granulated sugar
½ cup water
1 tbsp. glucose
¼ tsp. salt
1 tsp. vanilla extract
3 large egg whites
½ cup shredded coconut

Coffee & Walnut Cake with Brandied Prunes

1 Preheat the oven to 350° F. Put the prunes in a small bowl with the tea and brandy, and let stand for 3–4 hours or overnight. Grease and line the bases of 2 9-inch round cake pans. Chop the walnut pieces in a food processor. Set aside a quarter of the nuts. Add the flour, baking powder, and coffee, and blend until finely ground.

2 Beat the egg whites with the cream of tartar until soft peaks form. Sprinkle in one third of the sugar, 2 tablespoons at a time, until stiff peaks form. In another bowl, beat the egg yolks, oil, and the remaining sugar until thick. Using a metal spoon, alternately fold in the nut mixture and egg whites until just blended.

3 Divide the mixture evenly between the pans, smoothing the tops. Bake in the preheated oven for 30–35 minutes or until the top of the cakes spring back when lightly pressed with a clean finger. Remove from the oven and cool. Remove from the pans and discard the lining paper.

4 Drain the prunes, setting aside the soaking liquid. Dry on paper towels, then chop and set aside. Beat the cream with the confectioners' sugar and liqueur until soft peaks form. Spoon an eighth of the cream into a pastry bag fitted with a star tip.

5 Cut the cake layers in half horizontally. Sprinkle each cut side with 1 tablespoon of the prune-soaking liquid. Sandwich the cakes together with half of the cream and all of the prunes.

6 Spread the remaining cream around the sides of the cake and press in the chopped walnuts. Pipe rosettes around the edge of the cake. Decorate with walnut halves and serve.

INGREDIENTS
Cuts into 10–12 slices

FOR THE PRUNES:
1½ cups dried prunes, pitted
⅔ cup cold tea
3 tbsp. brandy

FOR THE CAKE:
4 cups walnut pieces
½ cup self-rising flour
½ tsp. baking powder
1 tsp. instant coffee powder (not granules)
5 large eggs, separated
¼ tsp. cream of tartar
½ cup plus 2 tbsp. granulated sugar
2 tbsp. sunflower oil
8 walnut halves, to decorate

FOR THE FILLING:
2½ cups heavy cream
4 tbsp. confectioners' sugar, sifted
2 tbsp. coffee-flavored liqueur

Wild Strawberry & Rose Petal Jelly Cake

1 Preheat the oven to 350° F. Lightly grease and flour an 8-inch, round, nonstick cake pan. Sift the flour, baking powder, and salt into a bowl, and set aside.

2 Beat the butter and sugar until light and fluffy. Beat in the eggs, a little at a time, then stir in the rosewater. Gently fold in the flour mixture and milk with a metal spoon or rubber spatula, and mix lightly together.

3 Spoon the cake mixture into the pan, spreading evenly and smoothing the top.

4 Bake in the preheated oven for 25–30 minutes or until well risen and golden, and the center springs back when pressed with a clean finger.

Remove from the oven and cool, then remove from the pan.

5 For the filling, beat the cream, yogurt, 1 tablespoon of rosewater, and 1 tablespoon of confectioners' sugar until soft peaks form. Split the cake horizontally in half, and sprinkle with the remaining rosewater.

6 Spread the warmed jelly on the base. Top with half the whipped cream mixture, then sprinkle with half the strawberries. Place the remaining cake-half on top. Spread with the remaining cream and swirl, if desired. Decorate with the rose petals. Dust the cake lightly with a little confectioners' sugar, and serve.

INGREDIENTS
Cuts into 8 servings

2½ cups all-purpose flour

1 tsp. baking powder

¼ tsp. salt

½ cup plus 2 tbsp. unsalted butter, softened

1 scant cup granulated sugar

2 large eggs, beaten

2 tbsp. rosewater

½ cup milk

½ cup rose petal or strawberry jelly, slightly warmed

¾ cup wild strawberries, hulled, or baby strawberries, chopped

frosted rose petals, to decorate

ROSE CREAM FILLING:

¾ cup heavy cream

1 tbsp. plain yogurt

2 tbsp. rosewater

1–2 tbsp. confectioners' sugar

Food Fact

Rosewater is distilled from rose petals and has an intensely perfumed flavor. It has been popular in the cuisines of the Middle East, China, and India for centuries.

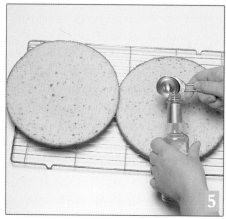

Celebration Fruit Cake

1 Preheat the oven to 325° F. Heat the butter and sugar in a saucepan until the sugar has dissolved, stirring often.

2 Add the pineapple and juice, dried fruits, and peel. Bring to a boil, simmer for 3 minutes, stirring occasionally, then remove from the heat to cool completely.

3 Lightly grease and line the base of an 8-inch, round springform pan with nonstick baking parchment. Sift the flour, baking soda, spices, and salt into a bowl.

4 Add the boiled fruit mixture to the flour with the eggs and mix. Spoon into the pan and smooth the top. Bake in the preheated oven for 1¼ hours or until a skewer inserted into the center comes out clean. If the cake is browning too quickly, cover loosely with foil and reduce the oven temperature.

5 Remove and cool completely before removing from the pan and discarding the lining paper.

6 Arrange the nuts, cherries, and prunes or dates in an attractive pattern on top of the cake. Heat the honey, and brush over the topping to glaze.

7 Alternatively, toss the nuts and fruits in the warm honey and spread evenly over the top of the cake. Cool completely, and store in a sealed container for a day or two to allow the flavor to develop.

INGREDIENTS
Cuts into 16 slices

½ cup butter or margarine

1½ cups dark brown sugar

13-oz. can crushed pineapple

1 cup raisins

1 cup golden raisins

½ cup crystallized ginger, finely chopped

½ cup candied cherries, coarsely chopped

½ cup candied peel, diced

2 cups self-rising flour

1 tsp. baking soda

2 tsp. pumpkin pie spice

1 tsp. ground cinnamon

½ tsp. salt

2 large eggs, beaten

FOR THE TOPPING:

⅔ cup pecan or walnut halves, lightly toasted

½ cup red, green, and yellow candied cherries

¾ cup small pitted prunes or dates

2 tbsp. honey

Tasty Tip

The fruit used in this cake will make all the difference in flavor—try to use natural candied cherries, which tend to have a fruitier taste. California prunes, seedless raisins, and golden raisins are usually more flavorful.

Toffee Walnut Swiss Roll

1 Preheat the oven to 375° F. Lightly grease and line a jelly roll pan with baking parchment. Beat the egg whites and cream of tartar until softly peaking. Gradually beat in ½ cup of the sugar until stiff peaks form.

2 In another bowl, beat the egg yolks with the rest of the confectioners' sugar until thick. Beat in the extract. Gently fold in the flour and egg whites alternately, using a metal spoon or rubber spatula. Do not overmix.

3 Spoon the batter into the pan and spread evenly. Bake for 12 minutes or until well risen and golden, and the cake springs back when pressed.

4 Place a clean dishtowel on a work surface, and lay a piece of baking parchment about 13 inches long on the towel and dust with confectioners' sugar. As soon as the cake is cooked, turn out onto the paper. Peel off the lining paper and cut off the crisp edges of the cake. Starting at one narrow end, roll the cake with the paper and towel. Transfer the cake to a rack to cool.

5 For the filling, put the flour, milk, and syrup into a small saucepan and place over a gentle heat. Bring to a boil, beating until thick and smooth. Remove from the heat and slowly beat into the beaten egg yolks.

6 Pour the mixture back into the saucepan and cook over a low heat until it thickens and coats the back of a spoon.

7 Strain the mixture into a bowl and stir in the chopped walnuts or pecans. Cool, stirring occasionally, then fold in half of the whipped cream.

8 Unroll the cooled cake and spread with the filling. Roll again, and decorate with the remaining cream. Sprinkle with the confectioners' sugar, and serve.

INGREDIENTS
Cuts into 10–12 slices

4 large eggs, separated
½ tsp. cream of tartar
1 cup confectioners' sugar, plus extra to dust
½ tsp. vanilla extract
1 cup self-rising flour

TOFFEE WALNUT FILLING:

2 tbsp. all-purpose flour
⅔ cup milk
5 tbsp. light corn syrup or maple syrup
2 large egg yolks, beaten
½ cup walnuts or pecans, toasted and chopped
1¼ cups double cream, whipped

Food Fact

Using a clean dishtowel to roll up the sponge in this recipe turns the steam into condensation, which helps keep the cake fairly flexible, preventing it from cracking.

Raspberry & Hazelnut Meringue Cake

1 Preheat the oven to 275° F. Line 2 cookie sheets with nonstick baking parchment and draw an 8-inch circle on each. Beat the egg whites and cream of tartar until soft peaks form, then gradually beat in the sugar, 2 tablespoons at a time.

2 Beat well after each addition until the whites are stiff and glossy. Using a metal spoon or rubber spatula, gently fold in the ground hazelnuts.

3 Divide the mixture evenly between the 2 circles and spread neatly. Swirl 1 of the circles to make a decorative top layer. Bake in the preheated oven for about 1½ hours until crisp and dry. Turn off the oven and allow the meringues to cool for 1 hour. Transfer to a wire rack to cool completely. Carefully peel off the papers.

4 For the filling, whip the cream, confectioners' sugar, and liqueur, if desired, together until soft peaks form. Place the flat round on a serving plate. Spread over most of the cream, setting aside some for decorating, and arrange the raspberries in concentric circles over the cream.

5 Place the swirly meringue on top of the cream and raspberries, pressing down gently. Pipe the remaining cream onto the meringue, decorate with a few raspberries, and serve.

INGREDIENTS
Cuts into 8 slices

FOR THE MERINGUE:
4 large egg whites
¼ tsp. cream of tartar
1 cup granulated sugar
¾ cup hazelnuts, skinned, toasted, and finely ground

FOR THE FILLING:
1¼ cups heavy cream
1 tbsp. confectioners' sugar
1–2 tbsp. raspberry-flavored liqueur (optional)
2½ cups fresh raspberries

Helpful Hint

It is essential when beating egg whites that the bowl being used is completely clean and dry, as any grease or oil will prevent the egg whites from gaining the volume needed.

Chocolate & Almond Daquoise with Summer Berries

1 Preheat the oven to 275° F. Line 3 cookie sheets with nonstick baking parchment and draw an 8-inch circle on each one.

2 Beat the egg whites and cream of tartar until soft peaks form.

3 Gradually beat in the sugar, 2 tablespoons at a time, beating well after each addition until the whites are stiff and glossy.

4 Beat in the almond extract, then using a metal spoon or rubber spatula, gently fold in the ground almonds.

5 Divide the mixture evenly between the 3 circles of baking parchment, spreading neatly into the circles and smoothing the tops evenly.

6 Bake in the preheated oven for about 1¼ hours or until crisp, rotating the cookie sheets halfway through cooking. Turn off the oven, allow to cool for about 1 hour, then remove and cool completely before discarding the lining paper

7 Beat the butter, confectioners' sugar, and cocoa until smooth and creamy, adding the milk or cream to form a soft consistency.

8 Set aside about a quarter of the berries to decorate. Spread one meringue with a third of the cream, and top with a third of the remaining berries. Repeat with the other meringue circles, cream, and berries.

9 Sprinkle with the toasted slivered almonds and the remaining berries. Sprinkle with confectioners' sugar and serve.

INGREDIENTS
Cuts into 8 servings

ALMOND MERINGUES:
6 large egg whites
¼ tsp. cream of tartar
1 cup plus 4 tbsp. granulated
  sugar
½ tsp. almond extract
½ cup blanched or slivered
  almonds, lightly toasted and
  finely ground

CHOCOLATE BUTTERCREAM:
6 tbsp. butter, softened
4 cups confectioners' sugar, sifted
6 tbsp. unsweetened cocoa, sifted
3–4 tbsp. milk or light cream
3 cups mixed summer berries such
  as raspberries, strawberries, and
  blackberries

TO DECORATE:
toasted slivered almonds
confectioners' sugar

Orange Fruit Cake

1 Preheat the oven to 350° F. Lightly grease and line the base of a 10-inch tube pan or springform pan with nonstick baking parchment.

2 Sift the flour and baking powder into a large bowl, then stir in the sugar.

3 Make a well in the center and add the butter, eggs, grated zest, and orange juice. Beat until blended and a smooth batter is formed. Turn into the pan and smooth the top.

4 Bake in the preheated oven for 35–45 minutes or until golden and the sides begin to shrink from the edge of the pan. Remove, cool before removing from the pan, and discard the lining paper.

5 Using a serrated knife, cut the cake horizontally about one-third from the top and remove the top layer of the cake. If not using a tube pan, scoop out a center ring of sponge cake from the top third and the bottom two-thirds of the layer, making a hollow tunnel. Set aside for a trifle or other dessert. Sprinkle the cut sides with the Cointreau.

6 For the filling, whip the cream and yogurt with the vanilla extract, Cointreau, and confectioners' sugar until soft peaks form.

7 Chop the orange fruits and fold into the cream. Spoon some of this mixture onto the bottom cake layer, mounding it slightly. Transfer to a serving plate.

8 Cover with the top layer of sponge cake and spread the remaining cream mixture over the top of the cake.

9 Press the nuts into the sides of the cake and decorate the top with the cherries, blueberries, and raspberries. If desired, dust the top with confectioners' sugar, and serve.

INGREDIENTS
Cuts into 10–12 slices

ORANGE CAKE:
2 cups self-rising flour
2 tsp. baking powder
1 cup granulated sugar
1 cup butter, softened
4 large eggs
grated zest of 1 orange
2 tbsp. orange juice
2–3 tbsp. Cointreau
1 cup chopped nuts
cherries, blueberries, raspberries, and mint sprigs to decorate
confectioners' sugar, to dust (optional)

FOR THE FILLING:
2 cups heavy cream
⅓ cup plain yogurt
½ tsp. vanilla extract
2–3 tbsp. Cointreau
1 tbsp. confectioners' sugar
3½ cups orange fruits, such as mango, peach, nectarine, papaya, and yellow plums

Chocolate Mousse Cake

1 Preheat the oven to 350° F. Lightly grease and line the bases of 2 8-inch round springform pans with baking parchment. Melt the chocolate and butter in a bowl set over a saucepan of simmering water. Stir until smooth. Remove from the heat, and stir in the brandy.

2 Beat the egg yolks and the sugar, setting aside 2 tablespoons of the sugar, until thick and creamy. Slowly beat in the chocolate mixture until smooth and well blended. Beat the egg whites until soft peaks form, then sprinkle over the remaining sugar, and continue beating until stiff but not dry.

3 Fold a large spoonful of the egg whites into the chocolate mixture. Gently fold in the remaining egg whites. Divide about two thirds of the mixture evenly between the pans, tapping to distribute the mixture evenly. Set aside the remaining third of the chocolate mousse mixture for the filling.

Bake in the preheated oven for about 20 minutes or until well risen and set. Remove and cool for at least 1 hour.

4 Loosen the edges of the cake layers with a knife. Using your fingertips, lightly press the crusty edges down. Pour the rest of the mousse over one layer, spreading until even. Carefully unclip the side, remove the other cake from the pan, and gently invert onto the mousse, bottom-side up to make a flat top layer. Discard the lining paper and chill for 4–6 hours or until set.

5 To make the glaze, melt the cream and chocolate with the brandy in a heavy-based saucepan and stir until smooth. Cool until thickened. Unclip the side of the mousse cake and place on a wire rack. Pour over half the glaze and spread to cover. Allow to set, then decorate with chocolate curls. To serve, heat the remaining glaze, pour it around each slice, and dot with cream.

INGREDIENTS
Cuts into 8–10 servings

FOR THE CAKE:

16 squares semisweet chocolate, chopped

½ cup butter, softened

3 tbsp. brandy

9 large eggs, separated

½ cup plus 2 tbsp. granulated sugar

CHOCOLATE GLAZE:

1 cup heavy cream

8 squares semisweet chocolate, chopped

2 tbsp. brandy

1 tbsp. light cream and white chocolate curls, to decorate

Food Fact

Wonderfully delicious served with a fruit compote— try making cherry compote using either fresh cherries, if in season, or otherwise canned in fruit juice. Pit the cherries, drain, and then simmer on a low heat with a little apple juice until reduced.

Chocolate Box Cake

1 Preheat the oven to 350° F. Lightly grease and flour an 8-inch square cake pan. Sift the flour and baking powder into a large bowl, then stir in the sugar.

2 Using an electric mixer, beat in the butter and eggs. Blend the cocoa with 1 tablespoon of water, then beat into the creamed mixture.

3 Turn into the pan and bake in the preheated oven for about 25 minutes or until well risen and cooked. Remove from the oven and cool before removing the cake from the pan.

4 To make the chocolate box, break the chocolate into small pieces, place in a heatproof bowl over a saucepan of gently simmering water, and leave until soft. Stir it occasionally until melted and smooth. Line a jelly–roll pan with nonstick baking parchment, then pour in the melted chocolate, tilting the pan to level. Leave until set.

5 Once the chocolate is set, turn out onto a chopping board and carefully strip off the paper. Cut into 4 strips, the same length as the cooked cake, using a large, sharp knife that has been dipped into hot water.

6 Gently heat the apricot preserves and strain to remove lumps. Brush over the top and sides of the cake. Carefully place the chocolate strips around the sides and press lightly. Let it set for at least 10 minutes.

7 For the topping, beat the cream to soft peaks, and quickly fold into the melted chocolate, along with with the brandy.

8 Spoon the chocolate cream into a pastry bag with a star tip and pipe a decorative design of rosettes over the surface. Dust with cocoa, and serve.

INGREDIENTS
Cuts into 16 slices

CHOCOLATE SPONGE:

1½ cups self-rising flour

1 tsp. baking powder

¾ cup granulated sugar

¾ cup butter, softened

3 large eggs

3 tbsp. cocoa

½ cup apricot preserves

cocoa, to dust

CHOCOLATE BOX:

10 squares semisweet chocolate

CHOCOLATE WHIPPED CREAM TOPPING:

2 cups heavy cream

10 squares semisweet chocolate, melted

2 tbsp. brandy

1 tsp. cocoa, to decorate

INDEX